EVERY CHILD DESERVES A MIRROR

REIMAGINING CURRICULUM THROUGH RELEVANT TEXTS

Written By:

Nadine A. Luke

© 2025 Nadine A. Luke

All rights reserved. This book or any portion thereof may not be reproduced in any form without permission from the copyright holder, except as permitted by U.S. Copyright law.

NJ Luke Publishing, LLC

Printed in the United States of America

The Library of Congress number: 2025921853

ISBN: 978-1-955202-20-6

Foreword

For far too long, schools have asked young people to read stories that never called them by name. They were tested on characters that did not look like them, settings that did not resemble their neighborhoods, and values that did not reflect their lived reality. The message—though unspoken—was clear: literacy belonged to someone else. The use of culturally relevant texts corrects that history and creates balance. They affirm identity before asking for achievement. They expand academic rigor by rooting learning in relevance, not by watering it down. When students see their families, languages, histories, joys, and complications reflected authentically on the page, reading becomes more than an assignment. It becomes a mirror and, hence, the reason for this book.

This text matters because it reinforces what we have long known. Students who do not see themselves in what they read often learn to erase themselves in how they think. It matters because diversity in books is not merely about representation—it is about access. In the article, "Steps to Authenticity: How authentic are your culturally relevant texts?" (Hollie, International Literacy Association, 2019), I say, "Ensuring access to texts that represent traditionally and historically underserved students should be a given, a basic right, not a choice or privilege." Culturally relevant texts also expand the horizon for all students, not only those whose stories have historically been omitted. They teach us that our collective story is always larger than a single narrative.

This book is both a call and an invitation—to teach in ways that honor identity, to curate texts that reflect lived experience, and to design classrooms where no student has to choose between academic success and cultural authenticity. With this book, the reader can change the possible to the probable, as it deepens our practice, challenges our habits, and reminds us that the use of culturally relevant texts is not a fad.

Sharroky Hollie, PhD.
Executive Director, Center for Culturally
Responsive Teaching and Learning

Table of Contents

Foreword..V

Chapter One:
The Problem With What We Teach..1

- Section One: The Story That Keeps Getting Told 1
- Section Two: When Representation Reinforces Harm..................2
- Section Three: When the System Becomes the Story 4
- Section Four: Whose Knowledge Counts? 6
- Section Five: Reflect and Reimagine..7
- Section Six: Disrupting Bias Through Belonging...........................9

Chapter Two:
Every Child Deserves a Mirror..15

- Section One: A Mirror Changed Me 15
- Section Two: The Mirror, The Window, and The Door...............18
- Section Three: The Cost of Absence 21
- Section Four: More Than Representation, Affirmation 23
- Section Five: Say It with Me—Every Child Deserves a Mirror ..26

Chapter Three:
From Books to Belonging 29

- Section One: The Science of Belonging...29
- Section Two: Literature as an Emotional Anchor 31
- Section Three: Classroom Culture Rooted in Representation ...33
- Section Four: When Literature Builds Bridges 36
- Section Five: Designing for Belonging..38
- Section Six: Reflection and Recommitment 40

Chapter Four:
What Culturally relevant Literature Looks Like 43

- Section One: Moving Beyond the Checklist..................................43
- Section Two: The Hallmarks of Culturally Relevant Texts 46
- Section Three: Stereotypes, Tropes, and What to Avoid 49
- Section Four: Evaluating Texts with Students and Families.......52
- Section Five: Booklists with Intention..53
- Section Six: Your Classroom as a Living Library 55

Chapter Five:
Opportunities for Student Voice 59

- Section One: From Silent Listeners to Storytellers 59
- Steps to Encourage Student Storytelling: 60
- Section Two: Designing for Dialogue..60
- Steps to Design for Dialogue: 61
- Section Three: Classroom Culture Rooted in Representation ...61
- Section Four: From Voice to Vision 62
- Section Five: Listening for What's Unsaid 63

Chapter Six:
Planning Engaging Lessons with Impact....................................67

- Section One: Where Intention Meets Practice.............................67
- Section Two: Designing Lessons That Center Identity and Voice 69
- Section Four: Differentiating With Purpose.................................70
- Section Five: Building Bridges Through Formative Assessment..73
- Section Six: Reflecting, Revising, and Rising................................75

Chapter Seven:
Responsive Teaching Practices That Center Students............79

- Section One: Teaching With Presence, Not Perfection...............79
- Section Two: Inviting Every Voice Into the Room 80
- Section Three: Creating Brave Spaces for Hard Conversations....80
- Section Four: Rethinking Assessment Through a Responsive Lens 81
- Section Five: Language That Heals, Not Harms.........................82
- Section Six: Reflecting and Reimagining in Real Time...............83

Chapter Eight:
Opportunities for Student Voice 85

- Section One: The Power of Voice in Learning.............................85
- Section Two: Storytelling as a Gateway..86
- Section Three: Choice as a Catalyst for Voice..............................86
- Section Four: Inquiry-Driven Projects...87
- Section Five: Making Space for Student-Led Discussion............88
- Section Six: Voice in Evaluation and Feedback..........................89

Chapter Nine:
Reimagine the System...91

- Section One: Systems Hold Stories..91
- Section Two: Auditing Curriculum With Purpose.......................92
- Section Three: Embedding Equity Into Professional Learning..93
- Section Four: Shifting the Role of Instructional Leadership......93
- Section Five: Creating Space for Student Partnership................94
- Section Six: Policies That Reflect Our Commitments................95

Chapter Ten:
What Culturally relevant Literature Looks Like 97

- Section One: More Than a "Diverse" Book...97
- Section Two: Texts That Invite Connection................................98
- Section Three: The Power of Joy-Based Texts.................................99
- Section Four: Text Makeovers 100
- Section Five: Cross-Content Connections.........................101
- Section Six: Bringing Texts to Life 101

Chapter Eleven:
Planning Engaging Lessons With Impact................................103

- Section One: Where Intention Meets Practice...........................103
- Section Two: Designing Lessons That Center Identity and Voice 104
- Section Three: Using Literature as a Launching Point 105
- Section Four: Differentiating With Purpose...............................106
- Section Five: Building Bridges Through Formative Assessment 107
- Section Six: Reflecting, Revising, and Rising................................108

Lesson Planning Templates and Supporting Materials..........111

Chapter One:

The Problem With What We Teach

Section One: The Story That Keeps Getting Told

Let me ask you this: When was the last time your curriculum made a child feel like they belonged? I mean *really* belonged, not as an afterthought, not as a sidebar, but as the heartbeat of the story?

"I realized I had mostly window books," one educator reflected during a workshop. "And the few mirrors I did offer were heavy with hardship. My Black students were starting to see their history only through chains and struggle, and even started joking, calling each other slaves. That broke me. I thought, 'What would it look like to give them joy? Imagination? A story that lets them be more than survivors?'"

Let that resonate.

We don't deny that stories of oppression matter. They do. But when we only tell stories of trauma, we fail to show the full humanity, complexity, and beauty of historically marginalized communities. We teach students that Blackness is synonymous with pain, that people of color are often painted only through struggle, that their identities are a monolith of model minorities, or exoticized caricatures. And all the while, we leave out Indigenous stories altogether.

Another educator shared this about her experience teaching Black history: "I used to read 'Henry's Freedom Box' every February. I told my students how he traveled upside down in a box for hours to escape slavery. They listened, and they responded well. But I had to be ready. You can't just pull these books off the shelf without preparation."

Exactly.

When the stories we tell center-pain without offering healing, joy, or empowerment, they become more about perpetuation than transformation.

And this isn't just about Black students. It's about *all* students. What do our classroom libraries teach our students about whose stories matter? What happens to a child who never sees their language, their traditions, their family structure, or their joy reflected in a book?

Section Two: When Representation Reinforces Harm

Representation without intention can reinforce harm.

It happens when we reduce identity to a single narrative. When we use stereotypes as shorthand. When we ask our students to "relate" to characters that were never written with them in mind.

Let me tell you a story.

British Indian author Sarwat Chadda once shared that a bookseller told him, "I don't see the point of stocking your book, we don't have any Indians in our neighborhood." Chadda's response. "I bet you don't have any hobbits, either."

Read that again.

We never question whether a child can relate to a wizard, a talking animal, or a dragon, but we suddenly become hesitant when the protagonist is Afro-Latinx, queer, neurodivergent, undocumented, or disabled.

Ellen Oh, co-founder of We Need Diverse Books, reminds us: "Even when diverse books exist, they're often the hardest for kids to access."

Why is that?

Bias. Assumption. The idea that some stories are niche while others are universal.

Let's name what's happening.

Bias shows up in the books we select, the stories we prioritize, and the authors we elevate. Research tells us that when educators operate under time constraints, stress, or fatigue, they rely more heavily on implicit bias (Bertrand et al., 2005). That bias shapes which stories we call "rigorous," which texts we assign, and how we interpret student engagement.

Take for example the ways we misread our students:

"She doesn't smile, so she must have an attitude."

"He speaks with slang, so he must not understand academic English."

"That student never participates, so he must not care."

Bias in action. And the data confirms it. According to the U.S. Department of Education, Black boys make up 18% of male school enrollment, but 41% of male school suspensions. Black girls make up 19% of female enrollment, but 53% of suspensions.

Our biases shape expectations. Expectations shape instruction. And instruction shapes outcomes.

Dr. Rudine Sims Bishop taught us that literature should act as mirrors, windows, and sliding glass doors. But in many classrooms, that mirror is shattered, the window is smudged, and the door is locked.

We must fix that.

Culturally relevant and responsive teaching is not just good practice. It's neuroscience. Zaretta Hammond reminds us that the brain functions best when it is safe, connected, and challenged. Culture is not a distraction from learning, it is the *way* we learn.

"Culture is to humans what water is to a fish," said Asa Hilliard. If you take the fish out of water, you don't just change its environment. You threaten its survival.

So let me ask you again:

What stories are we asking our students to swim in?

And what stories are we letting sink to the bottom of the shelf?

Section Three: When the System Becomes the Story

When we look at what's taught, not just *how* it's taught, it becomes clear that the curriculum itself tells a story. And far too often, that story centers-whiteness, marginalizes voices of color, and positions Euro-centric knowledge as the default.

We've been told curriculum is "neutral." But neutrality is a myth. Every book, every standard, every reading list is a product of human choice, and those choices reflect values, beliefs, and power.

Let's name it: The education system was not built with every child in mind. Equity is not a feel-good addition to our work; it's the work. As scholar Zaretta Hammond reminds us, minoritized students are navigating systems that were not designed for their success. That means equity is not about making things fair, it's about making things *right*.

So, how do we do that?

We begin by confronting the systems that elevate certain voices while muting others. Publishing statistics show that the majority of children's books are still written by white authors and feature white protagonists. Meanwhile, books by and about communities of color are often relegated to special months or themed corners of the classroom. This isn't just about inclusion, it's about healing historical harm.

The consequences are real. When students don't see themselves reflected in the curriculum, or worse, when they only see themselves reflected in struggle, their engagement, identity development, and academic performance all suffer. But when schools prioritize equity, diversity, and inclusion (EDI), the outcomes shift. Research shows that:

Students in racially and socioeconomically diverse schools demonstrate higher academic achievement (American Educational Research Journal, 2018).

Schools with strong EDI initiatives have higher graduation rates, particularly among historically marginalized groups (NCES).

Achievement gaps narrow when curriculum and instruction center equity (National Bureau of Economic Research).

This isn't hypothetical. It's measurable. It's real.

And it's happening in classrooms that have chosen to reimagine the system; In districts where students are identified not just as "struggling readers," but as *Learners of Standard English*. Also, in places where teachers are trained to recognize the brilliance in every dialect, every background, every story.

So let's stop pretending that books are just books. Let's stop pretending that standards are neutral. And let's stop asking students to check parts of themselves at the door to be considered "proficient."

When the system becomes the story, it's our job to rewrite it.

Section Four: Whose Knowledge Counts?

Let's pause and ask an uncomfortable but essential question: Whose knowledge gets validated in school? Who decides what counts as "important," "academic," or "appropriate" content?

When we ask students to memorize the Pythagorean Theorem but not the names of Indigenous lands, when we celebrate Shakespeare and silence Chimamanda Ngozi Adichie, when we praise fluency in English but penalize brilliance in African American Vernacular English, we are making choices. And those choices tell a story about what we value and who we believe is worthy of being seen.

In many schools, standard reading lists still consist of the same texts taught a generation ago. But culture is not static, and neither should our curriculum be. We must constantly ask: Are the texts we teach helping our students build schema that is relevant, affirming, and connected to their lived experiences?

This is where the concept of *cultural schema* becomes essential. Neuroscience shows that the brain retains and processes new information more effectively when it can link that information to existing knowledge, especially when it's culturally rooted. This is neuroplasticity in action. And it proves what educators like Asa Hilliard and Zaretta Hammond have always told us: Culture isn't an extra. It's foundational.

So what happens when we ignore that?

We ask students to leave parts of themselves at the door. We normalize a canon that glorifies colonialism and makes resistance invisible. We call students "below grade level" when in fact, they are brilliant, just not in the language or structure the test was built to reward.

And we send a message: Your ways of knowing do not belong here.

But here's the thing: they do.

They always have.

From oral traditions to dual-language households, from storytelling circles to code-switching brilliance, our students come into our classrooms fluent in culture. It's our job to meet them there.

So take a moment. Think about your curriculum. Think about your library. Think about your book clubs, your anchor texts, your read-alouds.

Whose knowledge are you centering? Whose voice is missing? And what would it look like to teach as if *every* child deserved to be seen not just in struggle, but in strength?

Section Five: Reflect and Reimagine

Before we move into frameworks and tools, let's ground this chapter in your lived reality. This is a moment to pause, not to critique others, but to reflect inward.

Reflection Prompts for Educators:

What is the racial, linguistic, and cultural makeup of your current classroom?

What percentage of the texts you use reflect the identities of the students you teach?

What messages, implicit or explicit, might students be receiving from your curriculum?

What stories are missing entirely?

Every Child Deserves a Mirror

How do your expectations for students shift based on their language, tone, behavior, or perceived attitude?

What books changed *your* life? Why?

Who chose the texts you currently teach, and who was left out of that decision?

Classroom Applications:

Conduct a "Library Audit" with your students. Have them sort your class texts into categories: Mirrors, Windows, and Sliding Glass Doors. What do they notice?

Start a conversation using book covers alone. Lay out the covers of 10–15 texts. Ask students: What do you think these books say about who and what matters in our classroom?

Ask students to write their own "I Am" poems or create a book jacket for a story that hasn't been written, but should be.

Introduce the Equity Illustration (Inequality, Equality, Equity, Justice) and connect it to your reading materials. Which books work toward justice, and how?

You don't need to overhaul everything overnight. But you do need to begin.

Because our students are already watching. They are already listening. They are already wondering where their stories belong.

Let's be the ones who answer with action. Let's be the ones who rewrite the shelves. Let's be the ones who say, clearly and unapologetically: Every child deserves a mirror.

Section Six: Disrupting Bias Through Belonging

Let's talk about what it really means to create an inclusive environment, not just one where students are present, but one where they feel powerful, seen, and centered.

Inclusion in the classroom is not just about what we teach, it's also about how we teach and how we respond to who is in the room. As educators, we are responsible for weaving diversity into the very fabric of our classroom culture, not as an occasional nod during a heritage month, but as a sustained practice that ensures no student feels isolated, misread, or overlooked.

In one of our workshops, I emphasized to the group that we have to forge a sense of belonging for all students. When we involve them in that process, when they help co-create the space, it changes everything.

Belonging isn't a feeling, it's a condition we create. Literature is one of our most powerful tools to make it happen.

But first, we need to take inventory.

Do your classroom texts reflect the identities of your students? Do they honor cultural and linguistic diversity, not just as "topics" but as lived experiences? Do they challenge stereotypes, disrupt assumptions, and invite students to see themselves and others in expansive, affirming ways?

When we fail to do this, we create room for harm to grow.

Let's name it: microaggressions and subtle discrimination are pervasive in schools. They're often unintentional, but they are never harmless. From the student whose hand is raised repeatedly but never called on, to the child asked again and again where they're "really from," these moments accumulate.

And they don't just hurt feelings. They impact academic performance, increase anxiety, and chip away at a student's self-worth.

But here's the good news, literature can help dismantle these harmful patterns. Culturally relevant books do more than reflect, they *interrupt* by:

1. Building Empathy and Understanding-Books offer windows into experiences that might otherwise be invisible. When a student reads about a character facing subtle discrimination, it can be a catalyst for deep conversation and reflection.

Example: A story about a child whose name is repeatedly mispronounced by their teacher can spark a dialogue about name-based microaggressions and the power of identity.

2. Challenging Stereotypes-Books can break open narrow narratives. When we offer texts where Black girls are scientists, where immigrant boys are poets, where students with disabilities are heroes, we challenge every single assumption students (and adults) might carry.

3. Providing Representation-For many students, the simple act of seeing themselves in a book is revolutionary. It affirms their presence. It elevates their story. And it tells their peers: *this child matters too.*

4. Encouraging Open Dialogue-Books become the bridge to conversations that are otherwise difficult to start. Stories give us shared language and safer entry points into topics like bias, race, identity, and justice.

5. Promoting Cultural Awareness-The more exposure students have to diverse perspectives, the more prepared they are to engage with difference, not as something to fear, but as something to respect.

6. Modeling Inclusivity-When teachers intentionally select inclusive books, they are modeling an ethic of care, curiosity, and equity. They set a tone for the classroom where all are welcome, and all are worthy.

But inclusion can't stop at literature. We have to also consider how we differentiate instruction so all students can access the meaning within those texts.

Differentiated instruction is equity in action. As Carol Ann Tomlinson reminds us, it's the belief that not every student needs the *same* thing, they need the *right* thing. And when we differentiate, we acknowledge the varied readiness levels, learning preferences, and lived experiences in the room.

Let's bring that down to earth with an example: A student does not need to know how to read at grade level to think critically. Maybe they need to *hear* the story, *act* it out, or *draw* what they understood. If our goal is comprehension, connection, and meaning-making, then we must offer multiple pathways to get there.

"Every student can learn, just not on the same day, or in the same way." – George Evans

Research backs this up. In John Hattie's *Visible Learning*, differentiated instruction has an effect size of 0.51, well above the hinge-point of 0.40, indicating significant positive impact on student outcomes.

So let's stop asking, *"Why can't they get it this way?"* and start asking, *"How else can I offer it so they will?"*

Quick Strategies to Support Inclusion and Access Through Literature:

Use audiobooks for students with processing or decoding challenges.

Create dioramas or posters to represent theme or character growth.

Let students doodle or annotate as they read, visual processing can aid retention.

Teach vocabulary proactively: Have students preview the text for unfamiliar words, define them in their own language, and share with classmates.

Reader's Theater: Invite students to act out scenes, using improvisation and emotion to deepen comprehension.

Use picture cards and visuals for multilingual learners or students new to English.

Change the ending: Let students imagine different outcomes and rewrite scenes.

Inclusion is not about lowering the bar, it's about removing the barriers.

Culturally relevant literature, paired with responsive, differentiated instruction, ensures that every student is invited to the table, not just to observe, but to contribute, to co-create, to belong.

This is the work.

It's not easy. It requires reflection, intention, and courage. But the payoff? A classroom where every child knows they matter. A learning space where difference is not something to overcome, it's something to *honor*.

So, as you close this chapter, I leave you with this: What will you do tomorrow to make your classroom a mirror?

And who might need to see themselves in the story you choose to tell next?

References

Bertrand, M., Chugh, D., & Mullainathan, S. (2005). Implicit discrimination. *American Economic Review*, 95(2), 94–98.

Bishop, Rudine Sims. (1990). *Mirrors, windows, and sliding glass doors. Perspectives: Choosing and Using Books for the Classroom*, 6(3), ix–xi.

Hammond, Zaretta. (2015). *Culturally responsive teaching and the brain: Promoting authentic engagement and rigor among culturally and linguistically diverse students*. Corwin.

Hilliard, Asa G. (2001). *Do we have the will to educate all children?* Educational Leadership, 58(7), 31–36.

Oh, Ellen. (2018, May 1). *Yes, we still need diverse books.* School Library Journal. https://www.slj.com/story/yes-we-still-need-diverse-books

U.S. Department of Education, Office for Civil Rights. (2014). *Civil rights data collection: Data snapshot (school discipline).* https://ocrdata.ed.gov

You begin by getting the kids engaged; then the academics can happen. The kids need to want to be at school, in the classroom, before they can learn.

- Dr. Sharroky Hollie

Chapter Two:

Every Child Deserves a Mirror

Section One: A Mirror Changed Me

I still remember the first time I recognized myself, really saw myself, in a book. Not just in a character's name or skin tone but in the rhythm of the language, in the cadence of the dialogue, and in the way a family gathers around a table loud with laughter and love and layered meaning. That story didn't just describe a fictional life. It described *mine*. And for the first time, I felt like the book wasn't trying to teach me something; it was trying to *hold* me.

But I also remember the years before that moment. When I flipped through pages of award-winning stories and couldn't find a single thread that tethered me to the text. When I was asked to write essays about protagonists who lived in worlds that looked nothing like mine. When I learned to translate my experiences into something more "relatable" before submitting a poem or a project.

That's the thing. When you don't see yourself reflected, you start to believe you don't belong.

And for many of our students, that's still their everyday reality.

Every Child Deserves a Mirror

A few years ago, a teacher I was coaching came to me with a concern about a student in her class, we'll call him Isaiah. She said, "He just won't read anything. I've tried everything on my shelf." In nearly every report she'd seen, he had been labeled a 'reluctant or non-reader,' described as disengaged, unmotivated, and apathetic.

We sat down together and talked about what was on her shelf. And more importantly, what *wasn't*. I asked her to consider whether any of those books reflected Isaiah's world, his voice, his rhythm, his brilliance. I shared some ideas for culturally relevant texts that might meet him where he was, stories with kids who looked like him, spoke like him and lived in worlds that made sense to him. These were stories rooted in joy, in resilience, and in everyday brilliance. Stories where the characters navigated real challenges but also laughed, dreamed, played, and thrived. I reminded the teacher that sometimes all it takes is one story that feels familiar, one mirror, to ignite something that's already inside a child, just waiting to be named and nurtured. I reminded the teacher that boys, especially Black boys, must also see strong Black girls.

A few weeks later, she came back to me lit up. "You won't believe what happened," she said. She had handed Isaiah *a* book that appeal to who he was as a person and his experiences; and for the first time all year, he didn't just read a few pages; he finished the whole thing. After reading the book, Isaiah started to open up. He told his teacher that he usually kept to himself because he didn't want to be teased about his hair or clothes. But this book gave them a bridge. It made space for connection, and slowly, a relationship began to grow, one built on understanding, not assumptions. He talked about it for weeks. And when he asked, "Do you have more like this?" that wasn't just a request for another story. That was a door swinging open.

That's the power of the right book at the right time.

Every educator I know has a story like this. Maybe it's the student who lit up reading *Hair Love* because they finally saw a dad who cared for curls like their own. Or the child who carried *They Call Me Africa* close to his heart because it told the story of a boy who was teased for his hair locks and dark skin but found strength through affirmations and self-love. That book didn't just tell his story. It helped him rewrite it with power and pride.

These are not just feel-good moments. They are *formative* moments. Because when a student finds a mirror in literature, it does something profound inside them. It affirms. It grounds. It liberates.

And let's be honest, it changes us as educators, too.

I've watched teachers weep as they read stories aloud and realized, maybe for the first time, how narrow the curriculum had been. I've seen their wheels start turning: *What else have I missed? What else can I bring in?* And I've watched classrooms shift from quiet compliance to joyful connection.

That's what happens when a story holds up a mirror. It doesn't just reflect, it transforms.

This work is not just about representation; it's about restoration. It's about giving students back what has too often been withheld from them: the right to see themselves as protagonists. As poets. As leaders. As loved.

And I want you to think about that.

When was the last time a book helped a student feel seen? When was the last time a book helped *you* see differently?

Let's not underestimate what's possible when a child walks into a classroom and recognizes that they belong, not because we told them they did, but because the shelves said so first.

Because every child deserves a mirror.

Section Two: The Mirror, The Window, and The Door

In 1990, Dr. Rudine Sims Bishop offered us a way to think differently about the role of literature in children's lives. She wrote that books could serve as mirrors, windows, and sliding glass doors. It's a framework that continues to shape how we think about equity, access, and affirmation in education, and it's a call to action we still haven't fully answered.

Let's unpack it.

A mirror reflects back to us who we are. It says, "I see you." For students, a mirror in literature means they can recognize their language, their family, their laughter, their neighborhood, and not just in the margins, but at the center of the story. It's a moment of being named and known. And as we've seen time and time again in classrooms, it's often the first spark toward loving reading, and by extension, loving learning.

A window offers a view into someone else's world. It lets us see what life might be like for someone who doesn't look like us, live like us, or believe what we believe. When we read with curiosity and openness, windows become tools of empathy. And in a time when division and misunderstanding seem louder than ever, cultivating empathy isn't a sidebar, it's the core of what it means to be an educated person.

A sliding glass door goes even further. It invites us to step into a new world, move around in it, learn from it, and return to our own changed. This is the power of story to transform. And that transformation doesn't end when the book closes. It walks with the reader into the next conversation, the next decision, the next relationship.

In one of our workshops, we explored what happens when classrooms consistently provide only one type of reading experience. One teacher reflected, "I realized I had mostly window books.

My students of color were always looking into someone else's life, and my white students were only seeing themselves."

Let that sit for a minute.

When we give one group mirrors and another only windows, we are teaching superiority and marginalization without saying a single word. We're reinforcing who gets to be centered, who gets to be celebrated, and who must always be looking in from the outside.

Now consider this: What happens when students get *none* of the three?

We heard stories from teachers who had students ask, "Why don't we ever read about people like me?" Or, more subtly, students who quietly disengaged from reading because they never found anything that spoke to their lives. This leads student to think, "If reading is always about someone else, it starts to feel like school isn't for me."

That is not an academic issue. That's an equity issue.

We must remember that culturally responsive literature doesn't just change what's on the shelf, it changes what's possible in the learning space. Students feel safer. They speak up more. They make connections more easily. Once we start using books that reflect our students' backgrounds, behavior issues decrease, and student engagement becomes amplified. They will stop seeing reading as punishment and start seeing it as a tool that opens up the world.

And let's be honest, this is about more than lesson planning. This is about access and equity.

To choose a book that reflects a student's lived experience is to say, "You are worthy of being seen. You are worthy of joy. You are worthy of being known." That's the heart of Dr. Bishop's message. And in a system where many students of color have only been shown literature that centers trauma, enslavement, and struggle, this becomes even more urgent. Yes, we teach history. But we must also teach humanity, and that includes stories of laughter, creativity, leadership, and resilience. It says this not just to students of color, but to all students. Because when white students read books where the protagonist is an Afro-Latinx girl, or an Indigenous boy, or a gender nonconforming teen, they're learning to expand their worldview. They're learning that *they* are not the default.

So let's ask ourselves:

What stories in our classroom act as mirrors?

What stories serve as windows?

And how often do we invite our students to walk through those sliding glass doors, and come back transformed?

Now let's ask the harder questions:

Whose stories have been missing?

Who's holding the pen, and who's being edited out?

Are we choosing stories that reflect deficit narratives, or ones that affirm brilliance and possibility?

Let this guide you as you continue reading. Because this is where transformation begins, not with the book alone, but with the belief behind it.

Every student deserves to see themselves not just in struggle, but in strength. Not just in pain, but in possibility.

And every classroom has the power to make that happen.

Section Three: The Cost of Absence

When students don't see themselves in books, the silence is louder than words. It's a kind of invisibility that speaks volumes: *You're not here. You don't matter.*

We see it in the child who used to raise their hand and now stays quiet. We see it in the student who rushes through reading logs or hides a book under the desk because they've learned that "those stories" were never meant for them. And we hear it in the sighs, in the shrug of the shoulders, in the dreaded phrase: "I don't like reading."

Let me be clear: our students do not hate reading. They hate reading about lives that feel disconnected, distant, or distorted. They are resisting invisibility.

And that invisibility comes with a cost, one we have failed to fully calculate.

In our workshops, we've heard it over and over again: students feel unseen.

Many students have expressed frustration that the only stories they encounter about Black people during Black History Month focus solely on slavery or struggle, often wondering why they rarely read about Black individuals simply living their lives, experiencing joy, love, and everyday moments without trauma as the central theme.

Let that sink in.

A student doesn't need to be able to name systemic racism to *feel* its weight. They can tell when the only stories about people who look like them begin with chains and end with civil rights marches. And yes, we must teach that history, but we must also teach the full spectrum of Black life, Latinx joy, Asian imagination, Indigenous wisdom, and Arab resilience. Our students deserve literature that affirms their brilliance, not just documents their oppression.

Asa Hilliard once said, "Culture is to humans as water is to a fish." So imagine asking a child to thrive in an environment that denies the very culture they breathe. That's what it feels like when curriculum fails to reflect students' lived realities. It creates a kind of educational dehydration, a thirst not for content but for connection.

This is where implicit bias creeps in quietly. When teachers select texts based on what they "always taught," when school libraries stock classics that reflect a narrow canon, and when reading levels are used as excuses to avoid culturally relevant material, we are unintentionally reinforcing the idea that some voices matter more than others.

And let's not ignore how this intersects with discipline. As we explored in our workshop, Black girls are the most suspended group in the school system, and one of the most common reasons cited? Attitude. What if what we label as "attitude" is actually a student reacting to years of exclusion; Years of having to code-switch, downplay their culture, or hear their name mispronounced every day? Literature can be a salve, a release valve, or a place to breathe.

One educator reflected, "After adding more inclusive books, my students started talking, about everything. They wrote more. They showed up differently. I realized the absence of mirrors had made them retreat, and those stories helped them engage more."

The cost of absence is not just lower reading scores. It's disconnection. It's mistrust. It's an internalized message that says, *your story doesn't count here.*

And here's the truth: when you erase a child's story, you erase part of that child.

This doesn't only affect students of color. When white students are always centered, when they are the unchallenged protagonists of every story, they develop a limited and distorted worldview. They come to believe their perspective is universal and everything else is supplemental. That mindset doesn't just live in books. It shows up in who gets called on, who gets recommended for honors classes, who's assumed to be capable.

The absence of culturally relevant literature feeds this imbalance.

We must shift. Not just add a few diverse books to the shelf, but transform our lens. Start asking:

Whose stories have we made visible?

Whose have we erased?

Who gets to be complex, curious, joyful, and ordinary?

This is not about checking a box. This is about repairing what's been broken.

Our students are telling us, sometimes in whispers, sometimes in behaviors, that they're paying that price every day.

And it's time we start listening.

Section Four: More Than Representation, Affirmation

Representation is important, yes, but let's be clear: it's just the beginning. Representation answers the question, "Do I see myself?" Affirmation goes further. It responds with, "Do I matter here?"

That distinction matters. Because we've all seen what happens when a student picks up a book that features someone who looks like them, but that character is reduced to trauma, tokenism, or a stereotype. That is not affirmation. That is harm wrapped in good intentions.

Affirmation means the character doesn't just exist, they thrive. They struggle, but they're not defined by their struggle. They succeed, but not because they had to overcome who they are. It's because they were rooted in who they are.

One of my students once said, "It's like in most books we're either slaves or superheroes. Can't we just be regular people too?" Let that sit. Because in between the extremes of pain and perfection is the rich, everyday humanity our students live. And that's what they need to see.

Affirmation means centering the complexity of identity. It's the child who is both soft and strong. It's the student who doesn't speak much in class but writes poetry that shakes the room. It's the girl who codes and cooks and sings and speaks three languages. When our literature reflects that richness, we're not just showing representation, we're offering validation.

Affirmation also means we are intentional about who is telling the story. It's not just about the characters, it's about the author's lens, their lived experience, their cultural proximity. Rudine Sims Bishop (1990) reminds us that literature should be more than a surface reflection—it should create a doorway into authentic worlds.

That's why we must ask not only, "Is this book diverse?" but also, "Who is holding the pen?"

In one workshop, an educator reflected, "I had a book about a refugee family, but when I looked closer, it was written by someone who had no connection to that experience. The kids knew it. They could feel it." That's what happens when authenticity is missing. Students can spot a surface-level story from a mile away.

When students read books by authors who share their language, their worldview, their rhythms and references, something clicks. The story feels like an embrace. A nod. A knowing. That's what we mean when we say the story is a mirror. It doesn't just reflect an image, it reflects truth.

Affirming texts don't hide cultural specificity, they lean into it. They let characters speak in African American Vernacular English (AAVE), or Spanglish, or Creole without translating it all into standard English. They let aunties be loud and grandmas be wise and uncles be complex and kids be everything in between. They show Muslim kids during Ramadan, Sikh boys tying their patkas, Native youth in ceremony and celebration. And they do so without apology or footnote.

In one workshop, an educator shared how her Latinx students lit up reading Me, Frida, and the Secret of the Peacock Ring. "It wasn't just that the main character was Latina," she said. "It was the food, the phrases, the way the family interacted. My kids didn't have to explain anything. They could just enjoy it."

Another teacher recalled a moment when a student saw a character with vitiligo and whispered, "She looks like me." That quiet recognition changed everything for her. Her shoulders relaxed. She joined the group. She wrote a story of her own.

That's the gift of affirmation. It says: You don't have to shrink to fit this story. This story makes room for you.

And it's not just for students who share the background of the characters. Affirming literature teaches all students that cultures are not caricatures. It opens their minds and hearts to nuance, to depth, and to common humanity in unfamiliar places.

Let's continue to embrace representation and affirmation by asking:

Are these stories written with authenticity?

Do they affirm students' identities, languages, histories, and dreams?

Do they challenge dominant narratives, or simply diversify the margins?

When a student sees themselves as the protagonist of a story, not just once, but regularly, they begin to internalize the idea that their life is worthy of literature. That their voice deserves to be heard. That their story is part of something bigger.

That is the work.

That is affirmation.

And that is how we begin to repair, to reimagine, and to reaffirm our students' place in the narrative.

Because every child deserves more than to be seen. Every child deserves to be celebrated.

Section Five: Say It with Me—Every Child Deserves a Mirror

So where do we go from here? We've explored what it means to see and be seen, what it feels like to walk into a classroom and know the stories on the shelves speak your name. We've talked about representation, yes, but also affirmation; real, full-bodied validation that tells students, "You belong here."

This final section is your invitation. To reflect. To act. To commit. This is your invitation to become what I call a mirror-maker.

Here are a few reflection prompts and classroom applications to help you get started:

Reflection Prompts:

When was the last time a student told you, "That book was about me." What book was it?

Think about your current classroom library or curriculum. Whose voices are amplified? Whose are missing?

Are the texts you're using affirming students' full identities, or only showing fragments?

How are students invited to bring their own stories into your space? Through writing? Speaking? Creating?

When students engage with literature, are they responding with compliance or connection?

Classroom Applications:

Conduct a bookshelf audit: Categorize your current texts by identity, voice, and genre. Make notes of patterns and gaps.

Use identity webs or cultural iceberg activities before choosing book club titles or read-alouds. Let students' lived experiences inform your text selections.

Invite students to write "book reviews for the soul," not about plot, but about how the book made them feel, what it reminded them of, or how it connected to their story.

Incorporate author studies featuring underrepresented voices, with a focus on how their backgrounds influence their storytelling.

Use literature circles with roles like "Culture Connector" or "Mirror Spotter" to help students engage with identity and experience intentionally.

Remember, this isn't about perfection. It's about purpose.

Say it with me: Every child deserves a mirror.

And every mirror deserves to shine.

References

Bishop, Rudine Sims. "Mirrors, Windows, and Sliding Glass Doors." *Perspectives: Choosing and Using Books for the Classroom*, vol. 6, no. 3, 1990, pp. ix–xi.

Hilliard, Asa G. "Do We Have the Will to Educate All Children?" *Educational Leadership*, vol. 58, no. 7, 2001, pp. 31–36.

Hollie, Sharroky. *Culturally and Linguistically Responsive Teaching and Learning: Classroom Practices for Student Success*. Shell Education, 2017.

Oh, Ellen. "Yes, We Still Need Diverse Books." *School Library Journal*, 1 May 2018, www.slj.com/story/yes-we-still-need-diverse-books.

Kautzsch, Alexander. *The Historical Evolution of Earlier African American English: An Empirical Comparison of Early Sources*. Mouton de Gruyter, 2002.

"Windows and Mirrors and Sliding Glass Doors: Ensuring Students See Themselves and Others in Literature." *Institute for Humane Education*, https://humaneeducation.org/windows-and-mirrors-and-sliding-glass-doors-ensuring-students-see-themselves-and-others-in-literature/.

Psychology Today. "Growth Mindset." *Psychology Today*, www.psychologytoday.com/us/basics/growth-mindset.

Tomlinson, Carol Ann. *The Differentiated Classroom: Responding to the Needs of All Learners*. ASCD, 2017.

Chapter Three:

From Books to Belonging

Section One: The Science of Belonging

Let's start with what we know: students do not learn when they do not feel safe. And they certainly do not thrive in spaces where they feel invisible or misunderstood.

Belonging is not a bonus. It is a biological necessity. Neuroscientist Zaretta Hammond (2015) explains that the brain is wired to seek safety and connection before it can process and retain new information. When a child perceives any kind of threat, whether physical, emotional, or social, the brain defaults to its survival mechanisms. That means students are more likely to operate in fight, flight, or freeze. They are not in a state to focus, collaborate, or think critically.

So what does that have to do with literature?

Everything.

When students see themselves reflected positively in curriculum, when they hear their language spoken with care, feel their cultural rhythms honored, or recognize their families, neighborhoods, and lived realities in the stories they read, their brains begin to relax. The sense of threat begins to dissipate. Students feel invited into the space rather than monitored by it. They lean in instead of checking out.

Affirming literature reduces the mental burden of "translation." Too often, students from culturally and linguistically diverse backgrounds are expected to constantly decode unfamiliar norms and values in their learning materials. This unspoken demand sends a clear message: school is not designed for you. But when students encounter stories that reflect their truth, that burden is lifted. Instead of thinking, "How do I fit into this world?" they begin to ask, "What can I build in this world?"

This sense of belonging is not just emotional, it is academic. According to research cited by Hammond (2015), culturally responsive teaching practices lead to deeper engagement and stronger information retention. When students feel safe and valued, their working memory improves, and their brains are more likely to engage in complex thinking. Simply put, affirmation feeds cognition.

One elementary educator in our workshop described the shift he saw in his classroom after introducing more culturally relevant texts. "I had a student who rarely spoke above a whisper. But the day we read a story about a family eating the same foods his family eats at home, he lit up. He talked about the spices, the way his grandmother cooks, the stories his father tells while they eat. His classmates asked questions. And just like that, he went from being silent to being seen."

That transformation did not happen by accident. It happened because he felt safe. He felt understood. And that is the foundation of learning.

Literature can be a tool for cultivating what Hammond calls a "warm demander" classroom, one where students feel deeply cared for and held to high expectations. It is not enough to teach standards. We must teach students. And that begins by building the kind of trust that allows students to take academic risks, share their ideas, and stretch beyond what they thought they could do.

Trust is built in small, consistent ways. Through stories. Through representation. Through language that embraces rather than erases. Through characters who are complex, full of contradictions, and worthy of compassion. When our shelves reflect that kind of diversity, our students begin to believe in their own possibility.

In our workshops, educators often share that students "come alive" when a character reflects their life. One middle school teacher told me, "I had a student who barely participated all year. But when we read a story about a kid living with his grandmother and speaking Spanglish, she couldn't stop talking. It was like the book opened a door she had been standing outside of."

That door is called belonging.

And literature can be the key.

Section Two: Literature as an Emotional Anchor

Equity in literature is not simply about offering access, it is about offering anchoring. According to the Chinook Fund (n.d.), "Equity is the moral imperative to provide access and support for all marginalized persons to realize their personal best; liberating all through the eradication of Ideological, Institutionalized, Interpersonal, and Internalized forms of oppression." In a school system not designed for over 90% of the students we serve, affirming literature becomes an act of equity. It becomes a lifeline.

Books are more than academic tools. They are emotional lifelines. They tether students to something deeper, something human. When the right story enters a student's world at the right moment, it does more than teach. It touches.

Every Child Deserves a Mirror

In classrooms where belonging is prioritized, literature often becomes the first bridge to emotional safety. Stories give language to feelings that many students, especially those carrying trauma or unspoken grief, may not yet know how to express. When a child reads about a character who is navigating abandonment, or grappling with identity, or finding joy in unexpected places, they do not just read. They recognize; and in that recognition, healing begins.

There was a high school English teacher who assigned a novel about a young boy dealing with loss. One of her students, who had recently lost a sibling, came to her after class in tears. Not because the book was too sad, but because, as the student said, "It finally gave me the words."

That is the power of an emotional anchor. It steadies students in when they are confused and feel they are isolated. It reminds them that they are not alone.

Books that mirror emotional truths also open the door to vulnerability. When students see characters cry, fail, apologize, or grow, it gives them permission to do the same. Social-emotional learning (SEL) is not a separate curriculum. It lives in the stories we choose, the conversations we foster, and the empathy we model.

Dr. Rudine Sims Bishop (1990) taught us that literature can be a mirror, a window, and a sliding glass door. But those mirrors must do more than reflect they must hold. They must be strong enough to help a child see themselves not just in the world, but in their own worth.

It is not just about sadness. Affirming stories offer joy too, the kind of joy that feels familiar. A girl giggling with her cousins at a family cookout. A boy quietly finding peace in his morning prayers. A teen finally feeling free in her natural curls. These are not small moments. They are soul moments. They remind students that joy is part of their story too.

In one workshop, I spoke about a time when I was reading a book that featured a Muslim child preparing for Eid. After the read-aloud, one student raised his hand and said, "That's what my family does." The student's whole posture changed. He sat up straighter. He smiled more. He was engaged. He even offered to bring in some of his books and artifacts so the students could see first hand what the book was talking about.

This is what we mean when we say literature affirms. It affirms that your life matters. Your story matters. Your emotions matter.

And once students feel held by a story, they begin to trust the space that offered it. That trust becomes participation. That participation becomes voice. And that voice? That becomes agency.

Section Three: Classroom Culture Rooted in Representation

Belonging is not something we can mandate. It is something we must nurture intentionally, consistently, and with deep care. And one of the most powerful ways to nurture it is through the collective culture we build in our classrooms. Representation is not just about the books on the shelves, but also about how students are invited to show up in the space.

Affirming literature can act as a cultural cornerstone, shaping not just what students read, but how they interact with each other and their learning. When classrooms are filled with stories that reflect multiple identities, languages, and lived experiences, the norms of that space begin to shift. A student who once felt unsure about raising their hand may feel emboldened after reading a character who sounds like them. A child who often sat alone may begin finding common ground through a shared cultural reference in a book.

Educators in our workshops have described noticeable shifts in behavior and engagement after integrating more culturally relevant texts. One teacher said, "My class went from silence to storytelling. Once students saw themselves in the literature, they saw the classroom as theirs, too."

This is not accidental. When students see that their identities are not only accepted but celebrated, they begin to bring their full selves to the learning process. Discussions deepen. Collaboration strengthens. Discipline issues often decline. Because when students feel like the environment honors who they are, they have less reason to disrupt it.

However, creating this kind of culture requires educators to be mindful about the messages their materials are sending. For example, in a reflection shared by Dr. Lindsay Pérez Huber (2022), a parent recalled reading a children's book that portrayed a stereotypical image of a "Mexican bandit," sombrero, serape, and sandals, used to explain a lie in the story. That image, subtle to some, was devastating to others. It reinforced bias, undermined trust, and failed to affirm the real lives of Latinx students and families.

This is why representation without reflection can do more harm than good. It is not just about having diverse books, it is about choosing *affirming* books. Books that reflect the dignity, complexity, and humanity of students' lives. Books that don't reduce cultures to costumes or trauma, but instead showcase the joy, brilliance, resilience, and everyday moments of being.

A culturally responsive classroom uses literature to shape inclusive norms. It invites students to speak in their natural voice, to question the world around them, and to see reading as a mirror and a megaphone. It opens the door to agency by showing students that their identities are not barriers to learning, they are bridges.

Representation is not just a mirror. It is the foundation of a classroom culture where students feel seen, heard, and valued. And when that happens, belonging is not just possible, it is inevitable.

So, what does this look like in practice?

Here are some actionable ways educators can create a classroom culture rooted in representation:

Literature Audits: Regularly assess your classroom library and curriculum. Ask: Who is represented? Who is missing? Go beyond checking off cultural boxes. Ensure books authentically reflect a range of experiences, voices, and identities.

Student-Centered Book Selection: Allow students to help choose read-alouds, literature circles, or independent reading materials. Use surveys, identity webs, or classroom conversations to find out what kinds of stories reflect their lived experiences.

Story-Based Circle Discussions: Create space for dialogue after reading. Pose open-ended questions that invite students to connect the characters' experiences to their own. Use discussion protocols that encourage every voice, especially those not always heard.

Visual Affirmation: Make classroom walls reflective of your students' identities. Include posters, artwork, and quotes from authors of color, cultural events, or student-created pieces. Display book covers that feature a range of backgrounds and bodies.

Cultural Responsiveness in Celebrations and Themes: Go beyond heritage months. Embed cultural stories, traditions, and experiences throughout the year. For example, read books about Black joy in March or Indigenous wisdom in April.

Representation in Author Voice: Highlight books by authors who share lived experience with their characters. Encourage students to explore how the author's background informs the story. Create "Author Study Corners" to deepen this exploration.

Affirming Writing Projects: Let students write their own narratives, drawing inspiration from books that reflect their world. Consider projects like "My Story in Six Words" or "If I Were in This Book."

Professional Growth: Engage in ongoing learning about implicit bias, culturally responsive pedagogy, and the intersection of identity and literacy. Reflect often, refine continually.

These strategies help shift classroom dynamics. They move us from compliance to curiosity, from managing behavior to cultivating identity. And they remind us that every decision we make, every book, every question, every interaction, either affirms our students or asks them to shrink.

Let's choose affirmation. Let's choose visibility. Let's build classroom cultures where representation is not a special feature, but the foundation.

Section Four: When Literature Builds Bridges

If a mirror helps us see ourselves, then a window invites us to understand others. And in classrooms, both are needed. While mirrors affirm identity, windows cultivate empathy. When done well, literature can serve both purposes at once, helping students to find common ground across lines of race, culture, language, religion, ability, and experience.

In one of our workshops, a teacher shared that after reading a book about a refugee experience, her students began asking questions. Real questions. Thoughtful ones. "Why did the family have to leave their home?" "What would it feel like to leave everything behind?" That conversation did more than explain displacement. It humanized it.

This is where literature becomes a bridge. Not just between characters and readers, but between classmates. Between neighbors. Between students who have never spoken to each other and now see something familiar in the stories they read.

But that doesn't happen automatically. It requires intentionality in how books are introduced and discussed. Simply assigning a book with a diverse character is not enough. Educators must create space for honest dialogue, and that means preparing students to enter conversations with humility, curiosity, and respect.

Classroom protocols can help. Literature circles that include roles like "culture connector" or "empathy builder" encourage students to look beyond plot and into perspective. Open-ended questions such as, "What part of this story reminded you of someone you know?" or "What surprised you about the character's choices?" can foster connection without forcing consensus.

Using a sliding glass door lens, as Bishop (1990) suggests, means helping students step into another world with imagination and integrity. When students read across identities, they must be taught to do so responsibly. This means we, as educators, must check our own assumptions and model what it looks like to engage with a story on its own terms.

This is also how we interrupt bias before it becomes behavior. If students only read about marginalized groups through stories of hardship, they begin to associate those identities with struggle. But when they see a Muslim protagonist fall in love, or an Indigenous teen ace a science competition, or a Black girl go on a space adventure, they begin to widen their lens. They begin to question the limits of the dominant narrative.

According to the Chinook Fund (n.d.), equity is about eradicating the ideological, institutional, interpersonal, and internalized forms of oppression. Literature helps do this by confronting stereotypes, humanizing differences, and promoting a sense of shared humanity. When students read stories that both challenge and connect them, they are learning how to coexist.

These moments matter. They are the foundation of classrooms that don't just teach tolerance, but model community. They are the groundwork for the kind of society we claim to want.

And it starts with a book.

A book that builds a bridge. A conversation that builds connection. A story that builds understanding.

Section Five: Designing for Belonging

Creating a classroom that fosters true belonging does not happen by chance. It is the result of careful design, ongoing reflection, and intentional practice. Belonging is cultivated in the day-to-day decisions teachers make about what is taught, how it is taught, and whose voices are included in the narrative.

Designing for belonging means we start by knowing our students, not just their reading levels or assessment data, but their identities, their communities, and the stories they carry with them. It means we view culture as an asset, not an obstacle. As Hammond (2015) teaches, our students come into the classroom with rich cultural schema that should be activated, honored, and leveraged as a strength in the learning process.

Teachers who design for belonging build environments that reflect the students they serve. They recognize that classroom walls, bulletin boards, and book displays send messages about who belongs. A teacher once shared with me, "I used to think neutral was safe. But neutral is often just coded for dominant culture." That shift in thinking prompted her to redesign her space with student artwork, family photos, multilingual signage, and culturally affirming book covers at eye level for her students.

This work also lives in the structures we create. Do we invite every student to speak, or do a few voices dominate discussion? Do our class jobs reflect a hierarchy, or do they reflect shared responsibility and value? Even small changes like offering students choice in how they respond to texts or present their learning, communicate that their voice matters.

We also design belonging through our classroom rituals and routines. Morning meetings that include identity check-ins, story circles that validate home languages, and journals that ask students to reflect on their experiences all help build a culture of connection. And these rituals do not have to take extra time. They can be woven into transitions, reading blocks, or exit tickets. What matters most is that they are consistent and sincere.

Importantly, designing for belonging also requires that we examine how we respond to behavior. Do we interpret a student's silence as defiance or as discomfort? Do we view a child's assertiveness as aggression or as self-advocacy? Research shows that Black and Latinx students, especially girls, are often disciplined more harshly for behaviors interpreted through biased lenses (Pérez Huber, 2022). To design for belonging is to commit to interrupting that pattern.

Equity-centered classrooms recognize that belonging is not just about comfort, but also about justice. As the Chinook Fund reminds us, equity involves dismantling ideological, institutional, interpersonal, and internalized oppression. And this dismantling must be built into the very architecture of our classrooms.

A classroom designed for belonging doesn't just celebrate culture during holidays. It builds a culture of inclusion, affirmation, and agency every day. It teaches students not only that they matter, but that they are essential. Not only that they belong, but that the space is incomplete without them.

Section Six: Reflection and Recommitment

Belonging is not just a pedagogical strategy. It is a human right. And as educators, we are stewards of that right. The stories we choose, the spaces we shape, and the relationships we nurture are all acts of either inclusion or exclusion.

This is where we pause. This is where we reflect. And this is where we recommit.

We reflect on the books we have been offering our students. Are they seeing themselves in these pages, or only learning about others? Are the stories reinforcing a single story, or are they expanding the narrative to include joy, resistance, creativity, and everyday brilliance?

We reflect on the systems and routines in our classrooms. Do our students feel trusted, or tested? Are they encouraged to speak their truth, or conditioned to remain quiet? Are we making room for their identities to thrive, or just to survive?

And we recommit to doing this work not as a one-time book audit, but as an ongoing practice of justice. To understanding that equity in literacy is not just a matter of access. It is a matter of affirmation. It is a matter of liberation.

Here are some reflection questions to guide your practice:

When was the last time a student told me they saw themselves in a book?

Whose stories am I centering in my classroom? Whose stories are missing?

How do my classroom norms reflect the values of inclusion, voice, and agency?

What assumptions might I be carrying into my book selections or discussions?

How am I continuing to grow in my understanding of culturally responsive and sustaining pedagogy?

And here is a simple, powerful reminder:

Every child deserves to walk into your classroom and feel like they matter. Every child deserves a story that says, "You belong." Every child deserves a mirror.

Let that be the legacy of your library. Let that be the heartbeat of your curriculum. Let that be the promise we carry forward.

References

Bishop, R. S. (1990). Mirrors, windows, and sliding glass doors. *Perspectives: Choosing and Using Books for the Classroom*, 6(3), ix–xi.

Chinook Fund. (n.d.). *What is equity?* https://chinookfund.org/equity/

Hammond, Z. (2015). *Culturally responsive teaching and the brain: Promoting authentic engagement and rigor among culturally and linguistically diverse students*. Corwin.

Pérez Huber, L. (2022, January 7). Racism in children's books is still an issue. *Latino Rebels*. https://www.latinorebels.com/2022/01/07/racismkidsbooks/

Literature transforms human experience
and reflects it back at us, and in that reflection
we can see our own lives and experiences as
part of the larger human experience.

- Rudine Sims Bishop

Chapter Four:

What Culturally relevant Literature Looks Like

Section One: Moving Beyond the Checklist

Let's start with an honest moment of reflection. Have you ever looked at a book, saw a character of color on the cover, and thought, "Perfect, this will add diversity to my shelf"? You wouldn't be alone. Many of us have reached for what we *hoped* was a culturally inclusive book, only to realize later it was more surface than substance.

This is not about blame, it's about growth.

We live in a time when the call for diverse books has become more visible, and that's important. But visibility without depth can be misleading. Just because a book features a character from a marginalized group doesn't mean it affirms that identity. Representation without authenticity can reinforce stereotypes, flatten identities, or worse, cause harm.

In one of our workshops, a teacher shared how excited she was to include a chapter book about a young Latinx girl. "It looked great at first," she said. "But as I read it more closely, I realized the story centered on assimilation. The 'happy ending' was the girl speaking perfect English and fitting in by hiding her home language. My students were confused. One even asked, 'Do I have to stop speaking Spanish to be successful too?'"

That question stayed with her. And it should stay with us.

Culturally relevant literature is not about checking a box. It is about offering a mirror that reflects students in their wholeness, language, culture, joy, pain, traditions, and dreams included. It is about choosing books that were written *for* our students, not just *about* them.

One key distinction is the author's perspective. Is the story being told by someone with cultural proximity to the characters? Do they speak from lived experience, or are they imagining someone else's world from a distance? Authentic voice matters. When stories are written from the inside out, they carry a resonance students can feel. It shows up in the dialogue, the setting, the values, the details no outsider would think to include.

This is where your role as an educator becomes more than just a curator of books. You become a guardian of identity. The stories you choose tell students what you believe about them and what you believe they deserve to see.

So let's move beyond the checklist. Let's commit to the kind of stories that don't just "feature" students of color, multilingual learners, or physically challenged kids, but center them. Let's choose books that reflect real lives, layered with complexity, dignity, and brilliance.

Our students don't need to be "included" in the story. They already are the story.

Our job is to make sure the literature we bring into our classrooms recognizes that truth.

As Dr. Rudine Sims Bishop (1990) explains, books serve as mirrors, windows, and sliding glass doors. When educators focus only on the outward appearance of a book's characters, they may provide a mirror that reflects back a distorted image, one that lacks depth or authenticity. Authentic representation must be rooted in real cultural experiences and written with a nuanced understanding of identity. One teacher I worked with realized this when a book about a Black family initially seemed affirming, but as she read further, it centered only on struggle and pain. Her students picked up on it, asking, "Is this all we are?"

This is where author perspective becomes critical. The #OwnVoices movement, popularized by We Need Diverse Books (n.d.), advocates for stories told by those who share lived experiences with their characters. These books reflect truth from the inside out. A third-grade teacher once shared how a book by an Afro-Latina author transformed a reluctant reader into a leader during literature circles. The student later said, "This feels like my abuela's stories." That connection was not coincidental, it was cultural alignment.

The research affirms what our students are already telling us. According to the National Education Association (2020), books that reflect diverse racial, religious, and economic backgrounds help build empathy and cultural understanding. This isn't just feel-good pedagogy, it's neuroscience and sociology. At the University of Wisconsin–Madison's Cooperative Children's Book Center, data revealed that less than 15 percent of children's books published in the last two decades include multicultural characters or stories (2020). The gap is clear, and it's our responsibility to close it.

Meanwhile, First Book's Diverse Books Impact Study (n.d.) found that when classrooms increased access to diverse books, students not only read more often but also for longer periods of time. Diverse books are not just tools for representation, they are catalysts for engagement.

If we want to foster a true culture of belonging and equity in our classrooms, we must be thoughtful about what stories are present, and just as importantly, which ones are not.

If we want to foster a true culture of belonging and equity in our classrooms, we must be thoughtful about what stories are present, and just as importantly, which ones are not.

Reflection prompt: Have you ever assumed a book was "diverse" just because the character looked different?

Difference between *diverse* and *culturally affirming* texts

Importance of author perspective, authenticity, and cultural proximity

Real classroom/workshop example of misrepresentation or unintended harm

Section Two: The Hallmarks of Culturally Relevant Texts

Once we move beyond surface-level inclusion, the next step is knowing what to look for. What actually makes a book culturally relevant? How can we, as educators, intentionally seek out texts that affirm and reflect the lived realities of our students?

Let's be clear: Culturally relevant books are not just those that *mention* a cultural element or feature a character of color. They are texts that engage culture authentically, portray identities with depth, and tell stories that resonate across lived experiences.

One of the clearest frameworks for understanding this comes from Dr. Rudine Sims Bishop's (1990) mirrors, windows, and sliding glass doors. Culturally relevant texts function as mirrors when they allow students to see themselves reflected with accuracy and care. They serve as windows when they help students look into lives different from their own. And they become sliding glass doors when students can enter a story with empathy, curiosity, and respect.

Let's take it further. The #OwnVoices movement reminds us that *who* tells the story matters as much as what the story is about. Lived experience adds authenticity and guards against flattening culture into caricature. It's the difference between a story that feels like an invitation and one that feels like an explanation.

So what should we be looking for?

Authentic representation: Characters feel real. They are shaped by culture, not defined solely by it.

Nuanced characters: Identities are layered. A Black girl can be brilliant, silly, angry, joyful, and everything in between, within the same book.

Cultural specificity: The setting, traditions, language, and experiences are not generic. They reflect real communities, down to the food on the table or the way a grandma ties her scarf.

Complex, multidimensional identities: Characters are more than their trauma or challenges. They are shown in moments of joy, growth, friendship, and agency.

Balance of joy and struggle: Culturally relevant texts include stories of resistance, yes. But they also celebrate culture, resilience, and everyday life. As one student once said after reading a story centered on joy, "This book is different. It reminded me so much of my own home."

In our workshops, we often show side-by-side examples of two books that both feature a protagonist from a marginalized background. One might check a diversity box, but flatten the character's identity. The other centers the character in a fully realized world with dreams, family, flaws, and brilliance.

That's what we're aiming for. Books that affirm and expand. Books that allow students to see who they are, and who they can become.

Because when students read stories that reflect their whole selves, they are reminded that they belong. And when they read stories that honor the full lives of others, they become more capable of empathy, compassion, and connection.

Recent research supports these observations. A study highlighted by the Iowa Reading Research Center (2022) found that culturally relevant texts help students form stronger connections to characters, which improves comprehension and engagement. Similarly, Edutopia (2020) emphasizes that the right books can help students explore different perspectives, building empathy across lines of difference. For English learners in particular, Renaissance Learning (2018) notes that culturally appropriate materials can accelerate language acquisition by providing emotional connection and context. These are not just theoretical benefits. They show up in real classrooms every day.

Frameworks: Bishop's mirrors/windows/sliding glass doors, #OwnVoices

What to look for:

Authentic representation

Nuanced characters

Cultural specificity

Complex, multidimensional identities

Stories of joy, resilience, and everyday life—not just trauma

Examples across grade levels

Section Three: Stereotypes, Tropes, and What to Avoid

Not every book that features a character from a marginalized background is culturally relevant. Some do more harm than good, even if the intent is well-meaning. If we're not careful, we can unknowingly bring stories into our classrooms that reinforce outdated, harmful, or incomplete ideas about students and their communities.

I once read a children's book where the only Black character was either saving the day with magical powers or sacrificing themselves for the white protagonist's growth. Another time, I saw an "empowerment" story that reduced a character's culture to a few bold colors and a food item. It looked bright and affirming at a glance, but on closer reading, it leaned into caricature rather than complexity.

These are not isolated incidents. As Lindsay Pérez Huber (2022) points out in her article for Latino Rebels, stereotypical imagery, like the outdated "Mexican bandit" trope, is still present in modern children's books. In her story, a well-intentioned book used a sombrero-wearing character as the punchline of a child's lie. What message does that send to a young Latinx reader? To their peers?

Here are a few of the most common harmful tropes to watch for, especially when examining how Black and Brown characters are portrayed in children's literature:

The trauma-only narrative: Stories that only center struggle, oppression, or survival. While these realities are important, they should not be the sole representation. Black children, for example, should not have to wade through a canon of books that only highlight enslavement, incarceration, or systemic failure before encountering stories of joy, creativity, or excellence.

The magical or wise sidekick: Often, characters of color are positioned only to support the growth of the white protagonist. They appear wise or mystical but lack full development.

The model minority: Portraying students from certain backgrounds (especially Asian and immigrant communities) as uniformly high-achieving, quiet, or compliant. This flattens identity and places harmful pressure on students.

The mischievous or criminal Black boy: Repeated depictions of Black boys as deceptive, dishonest, or inherently in trouble reinforce damaging racial stereotypes. These portrayals normalize deficit thinking and can shape how Black boys are perceived and treated in classrooms.

The "loud" or "fast" Black girl: When Black girls are depicted as sassy, back-talking, or overly sexualized, whether intentionally or not, it plays into historical tropes that rob them of innocence and humanity. Even stories meant to highlight strength can fall into this trap if not handled with care.

The absentee or criminalized Black father: Too often, Black family structures are portrayed as broken by default, with fathers either absent, incarcerated, or ineffective. This not only distorts reality, it sends a message to students that loving, stable Black fatherhood is an exception rather than the norm.

The angry or dismissive Black woman: Sometimes embedded in matriarch-only households, Black women are cast as demeaning or emotionally distant, often to uplift white or male characters. Without balance, this narrative reinforces harmful ideas about who Black women are allowed to be.

When these tropes show up in books, students internalize the messages. Some may feel erased or stereotyped. Others may walk away with a skewed or shallow understanding of their peers' lived experiences.

So how do we spot these issues before they hit our shelves?

Ask who the book centers: Whose voice drives the story? Whose emotions and perspective take up the most space?

Check for complexity: Are the characters fully human, with hopes, contradictions, humor, and depth? Or do they fall into predictable patterns?

Question intent and impact: Even if the book was meant to teach a lesson, what unintended lessons might it also carry?

Use trusted tools: Resources like the Diverse BookFinder, the American Indian Library Association, and #DisruptTexts provide critical reviews and guides to help navigate this work.

This is about more than avoiding harm. It's about offering students the kind of literature that truly sees them. That honors the fullness of who they are. That tells the truth but tells the whole truth.

Because our students deserve more than representation. They deserve respect.

Case study: Pérez Huber's (2022) article on stereotypes in children's books

- Define common harmful tropes:
- Trauma-only narratives
- Magical or wise "sidekick" figures
- Model minority myths
- Tools for critical evaluation and questions to ask

Section Four: Evaluating Texts with Students and Families

Culturally relevant literature isn't just something we hand to students, it's something we explore with them. When students are involved in the process of selecting, evaluating, and reflecting on the books they read, we open the door to deeper learning, richer conversations, and stronger connections.

We start with a simple shift: Instead of asking "Do they like this book?" we ask, "Do they see themselves in this book?" and "How does this story shape the way they see others?"

One educator shared a moment when her class finished reading a picture book that centered a multi-generational Black family. After the last page, a student quietly said, "That's my house. We do that too." That single moment sparked a class discussion about family, culture, and memory. All because the teacher chose to ask, "What did this story make you think about in your own life?"

Evaluating texts with students does not mean turning your classroom into a literary criticism seminar. It means inviting students to reflect out loud. It means asking questions like:

Who do you think this book was written for?

Did anything in this story feel familiar or unfamiliar?

How did the characters remind you of people you know, or don't know?

What did this book make you feel, and why?

These aren't just reading comprehension questions. They're identity-building questions. They create space for students to name their experiences, challenge bias, and expand their understanding of others.

Families are essential partners in this work. Inviting families to share the stories that are meaningful in their homes—whether from oral traditions, books in other languages, or community-specific experiences, adds texture and authenticity to the classroom library. When a student sees a book their family recommended on the shelf, they understand that their voice matters in this space.

You can create space for this by:

- Sending home book surveys or "family story" prompts
- Hosting book tastings where students and families preview diverse texts together
- Inviting families to recommend stories in their home languages or from their cultural background
- Creating bulletin boards that showcase "Books We Love at Home"
- Evaluating literature alongside students and families builds more than a booklist, it builds trust. It signals to students that their perspectives are valid, their cultures are valued, and their stories belong in our classrooms.

And that is how we move from inclusion to transformation, one shared story at a time.

How to co-evaluate books with students

Collecting feedback on representation and relatability

Partnering with families to include multilingual and culturally grounded stories

Literacy as relationship-building

Section Five: Booklists with Intention

Selecting the right books for your classroom library is not just a logistical task, it is a pedagogical and moral commitment.

Every Child Deserves a Mirror

The books we offer our students shape not only how they see the world, but how they see themselves and others. Curating a thoughtful, intentional booklist helps ensure that every student can find stories that reflect their identities, expand their horizons, and affirm their experiences.

When building a classroom collection, it is important to draw from trusted sources and prioritize voices that speak authentically to the lived realities of your students. Excellent resources include We Need Diverse Books, HipLatina, Black Children's Book Week, Malik Books (Los Angeles), and community libraries that center BIPOC and marginalized authors. These organizations and outlets prioritize books that go beyond tokenism, offering stories rich in culture, nuance, and affirmation.

As you develop or revise your booklist, consider the following guiding questions:

Who is represented? Look beyond surface traits like skin color or cultural markers. Are the characters' lives, values, and experiences authentically portrayed? Do they reflect the diversity within cultural groups, not just between them?

Who is telling the story? Seek out #OwnVoices authors and creators with cultural proximity to the characters and communities they portray. Authentic authorship leads to richer, more accurate storytelling.

Does the book affirm or flatten identity? Avoid books that reduce characters to stereotypes or frame marginalized identities solely through struggle. Look for texts that highlight joy, complexity, resilience, and growth.

Additionally, strive for variety across genres, themes, and reading levels. Include:

Contemporary stories and historical narratives

Fiction, nonfiction, poetry, and graphic novels

Stories centered on joy, resilience, creativity, and identity

A fifth-grade teacher in one of our workshops shared how she introduced a new graphic novel series featuring a biracial protagonist who loved science fiction. "I had students who never picked up a book voluntarily suddenly asking for the next one in the series," she said. "They saw themselves not only in the character's background but in his curiosity and imagination."

This is the power of a well-curated library. It invites students not just to read, but to see possibilities. It tells them, "Your stories matter here."

And when students believe their stories matter, they become more willing to engage with the stories of others. That is where empathy grows. That is where learning deepens. That is where belonging takes root.

Age/grade-based curated examples:

Trusted sources: We Need Diverse Books, HipLatina, Black Children's Book Week, Malik Books (Los Angeles), and community libraries

Questions to guide curation:

- Who is represented?
- Who is telling the story?
- Does it affirm or flatten identity?

Section Six: Your Classroom as a Living Library

A classroom library should never be a static collection of books gathering dust on a shelf. It should be a dynamic, living resource that evolves alongside the students it serves. Just as students grow, change, and explore new facets of their identities, so too should the literature we provide.

First, think of the library as a conversation starter, not a closed set of materials. Curate books that invite dialogue and reflection. Make rotating titles a regular practice. As new voices emerge in publishing, add them. When students share interests or questions that surface during class discussions, seek out literature that speaks to those topics.

I always recommend teachers to begin rotating books monthly based on student interests, cultural events, and family contributions. A workshop participant noted, "When students started seeing new books show up that reflected what we had been talking about, they felt heard," she said. "They also started recommending books for each other. The library became a shared space, not just my collection."

Second, make student voices a cornerstone of the library's evolution. Invite students to suggest books they love or want to explore. Include family voices by asking caregivers to share stories from their backgrounds or recommend authors and books meaningful to their communities. This partnership extends the library beyond the classroom walls and reinforces the idea that literacy is a shared journey.

Accessibility is just as important as representation. Place books where students can easily browse and touch them. Use bins, face-out displays, and clear labeling. Ensure books are available at a variety of reading levels and in multiple languages when possible. When students see books that are visible, inviting, and reflective of their realities, they are more likely to engage.

Finally, celebrate the library as a space of belonging. Host book talks, reading circles, and author studies. Highlight student reviews and book recommendations on a classroom bulletin board. Make literature not just an academic requirement, but a lived experience that fosters curiosity, identity exploration, and joyful learning.

A living library is more than a collection. It is a statement. It says to every student who walks through your door: You belong here. Your story matters. And you are a vital part of this learning community.

Treat the classroom bookshelf as a dynamic space

Rotating and updating books

Including student recommendations and family voices

Making literature accessible, visible, and celebrated

References

Bishop, R. S. (1990). *Mirrors, windows, and sliding glass doors. Perspectives: Choosing and Using Books for the Classroom*, 6(3), ix–xi.

Cooperative Children's Book Center. (2023). *Books by and About Black, Indigenous and People of Color 2023*. University of Wisconsin–Madison.

Pérez Huber, L. (2022, January 7). *Racism in children's books is still an issue.* Latino Rebels. https://www.latinorebels.com/2022/01/07/racismkidsbooks/

I think it's important for us to help students keep the big picture in mind, and not to define themselves soley in those not-so-ideal terms.

- Dr. Tyrone Howard

Chapter Five:

Opportunities for Student Voice

Section One: From Silent Listeners to Storytellers

Let's start with a classroom moment. A student raises her hand. Her voice shakes a little as she begins to speak, but her words are clear. "This story reminds me of my grandmother. She used to tell me stories just like this, about when she came here from another country." The room shifts. Suddenly, the story is not just about the character in the book. It's about *her*. It's about *us*.

That's the power of voice.

For too long, student voice has been treated as an add-on, something extra if there's time. But voice is not a luxury. It's a cornerstone of equity. When students speak, they are not just participating; they are *belonging*. And when we center their voices, we are affirming that their experiences, cultures, and ways of knowing are essential to the learning space.

According to the First Book (2023) Diverse Books Impact Study, classrooms that incorporate student voice and culturally relevant content increase motivation, time spent reading, and overall academic engagement. When students see their language, identity, and culture reflected in both the curriculum and classroom discourse, they feel valued. The National Education Association (NEA, 2020) also notes that engaging students in dialogue about their lived experiences fosters empathy, classroom connectedness, and critical thinking.

Steps to Encourage Student Storytelling:

Introduce Identity Reflections: Use journals or visual prompts to invite students to reflect on aspects of their background and interests.

Start with Mentor Texts: Choose books where young people share their own stories. Model the connection between literature and lived experience.

Validate Multiple Forms of Expression: Allow students to share stories through visuals, music, oral narrative, or other modalities.

Create a Classroom Agreement: Establish norms for listening, confidentiality, and respect to ensure safety in storytelling spaces.

Section Two: Designing for Dialogue

Creating space for student voice begins with intentional design. It starts with the questions we ask and the platforms we provide for expression.

Think about the kinds of prompts you use. Are they open-ended? Do they invite connection to identity, community, and culture? A question like, "What would you have done in this situation?" is fine. But, "How does this connect to your own experiences or the stories in your family?" invites deeper reflection and relevance.

In culturally responsive classrooms, educators design with dialogue in mind. According to Renaissance Learning (2018), students engage more deeply with texts when they have opportunities to respond in ways that reflect their linguistic and cultural strengths. Dialogue is not just a method, it's a mindset.

Steps to Design for Dialogue:

Use Texts with Built-in Discussion Points: Choose stories that reflect social justice themes, identity conflicts, or cultural celebrations.

Teach Discussion Structures: Introduce students to Socratic seminar, fishbowl discussion, and literature circles to build confidence.

Assign Discussion Roles: Help students develop speaking and listening skills by rotating roles such as summarizer, connector, and questioner.

Include Self and Peer Reflection: After discussions, allow students to reflect on how their thinking evolved or how they felt during the dialogue.

Section Three: Classroom Culture Rooted in Representation

A culture of voice begins with a culture of trust. When students see that their identities are reflected in the books they read, the walls of the classroom, and the norms of discussion, they are more likely to share openly.

Start by co-creating community agreements. Invite students to define what respectful dialogue looks like. Discuss what it means to disagree without dismissing. Normalize multiple truths. Validate multiple Englishes.

Model vulnerability. Share your own reflections. Talk about when a story moved you or challenged you. Students are more likely to open up when they see that learning is a shared, human experience.

Highlight authors and stories that reflect the diversity of your classroom. The University of Wisconsin–Madison (2020) reports that less than 15% of children's books published over the past

Every Child Deserves a Mirror

two decades include multicultural characters or themes. Representation in classroom libraries is essential.

Steps to Root Classroom Culture in Representation:

Audit Your Library and Curriculum: Assess whether students see themselves in the texts and authors presented.

Invite Family and Community Input: Ask families what stories matter in their culture and home language.

Display Student Work: Showcase diverse identities through student-created identity maps, poems, and artwork.

Highlight Linguistic Diversity: Celebrate home languages and dialects through multilingual displays, dual-language books, and affirming classroom norms.

Section Four: From Voice to Vision

Let's continue to embrace representation by asking: How are students shaping the curriculum? Are they choosing the texts? Designing the projects? Evaluating the learning?

Co-evaluation is a powerful way to honor student voice. After a unit, invite students to reflect on the materials: Did you see yourself in these stories? What felt missing? What would you add?

Invite families to be part of this visioning process. Ask them what stories matter in their homes, what authors they recommend, what languages they'd love to see represented. This isn't just about inclusion, it's about transformation.

Research from Edutopia (2020) underscores that students who co-construct learning experiences develop higher-order thinking skills, greater motivation, and a stronger sense of ownership in their learning.

Steps to Move from Voice to Vision:

Use Student Feedback Surveys: Ask students to evaluate text choice, engagement, and inclusion.

Incorporate Student-Led Conferences: Empower students to share progress and goals through their own lens.

Launch Inquiry Projects: Let students choose topics that matter to them, framed around essential questions.

Facilitate Curriculum Audits: With older students, analyze whose voices are centered—and whose are missing.

Section Five: Listening for What's Unsaid

Some students will jump into discussions headfirst. Others will hold back. And that's okay. Our job is not to force voice, but to make space for it, to listen for what's unspoken and to create the conditions for every student to feel safe enough to speak.

I once taught a student who was bright, fluent, and engaged in every small group activity. But when it came time to write reflections or share out loud, she'd freeze. Through one-on-one conversations, I learned that she had internalized the belief that her thoughts didn't sound "smart enough." Her dialect, her sentence structures, her way of seeing the world had been dismissed in previous classrooms.

So we worked on reframing that narrative. We talked about the power of storytelling in her community. We read texts that reflected her linguistic style. We practiced responding to literature through dialogue instead of formal essays. Over time, she found her voice again, and it was beautiful.

Research supports this practice. CASEL (2023) and NEA (2020) highlight that affirming a student's identity through language and expression increases engagement and builds academic confidence.

Steps to Listen for the Unspoken:

Build Relationships First: Use consistent check-ins and conferences to know students beyond academics.

Recognize Nonverbal Expression: Look for engagement in art, body language, and participation style.

Use Scaffolds for Communication: Offer sentence frames, visuals, or partner shares to support emerging voices.

Affirm Home Cultures and Speech: Create space where all language patterns are recognized as valid and valuable.

This is the work. Not just making room for voice, but helping students reclaim it.

Because voice is not volume. It's value. It's knowing that your truth matters.

And when every student knows that, they don't just read the story.

They write it.

References

CASEL. (2023). *What is SEL?* Collaborative for Academic, Social, and Emotional Learning. https://casel.org

Edutopia. (2020, October 28). *How student voice can lead to deeper learning.* George Lucas Educational Foundation. https://www.edutopia.org/article/how-student-voice-can-lead-deeper-learning

First Book. (2023). *Diverse books impact study.* First Book Research & Insights. https://firstbook.org/research

National Education Association. (2020). *Student voice: A growing movement within education that benefits students and teachers.* NEA. https://www.nea.org

Renaissance Learning. (2018). *What kids are reading: 2018 edition. Renaissance.* https://www.renaissance.com/edwords/what-kids-are-reading

University of Wisconsin–Madison, Cooperative Children's *Book Center.* (2020). *Books by and about Black, Indigenous and People of Color 2019 publishing statistics. CCBC.* https://ccbc.education.wisc.edu

You don't just teach, you inspire!

-Dr. Marcia Tate

Chapter Six:

Planning Engaging Lessons with Impact

Section One: Where Intention Meets Practice

Representation in literature is only the beginning. According to research from the NEA Foundation (2024), when students engage with literature that reflects their identities and experiences, their academic outcomes and classroom participation improve significantly. The real magic happens when we build intentional, culturally relevant lessons around the books we bring into our classrooms. This is where theory becomes action, and stories move from the page into the hearts, minds, and lives of students.

Let's start here: A great book is a spark, not the whole fire. It's the educator's role to fan that flame, to create learning experiences that encourage deep thinking, reflection, and connection. But to do that well, we must move beyond compliance-driven lesson plans and into practices that honor student identity, voice, and agency. As Bradshaw et al. (2018) emphasize, culturally responsive classroom strategies, including identity-affirming lesson plans, result in higher student engagement and reduced disciplinary issues, especially among historically marginalized students.

Culturally responsive lesson design begins with knowing your students. Not just their reading levels or test scores, but their stories, cultures, home languages, learning styles, and lived experiences. When we know who our students are, we can build lessons that speak directly to them, lessons that affirm their brilliance while challenging them to grow.

Traditional paragraph-style reading response prompts often present barriers for multilingual learners, who may have rich ideas but struggle with standardized writing formats. Instead, consider using visual journals, combining drawings, key vocabulary in both English and home languages, and creative expression through song lyrics or personal reflections. This approach creates a more inclusive space where students can demonstrate understanding and connect emotionally with texts. Renaissance Learning (2018) found that when English learners are provided with culturally appropriate and multi-modal instructional materials, they demonstrate increased comprehension, engagement, and academic success. These strategies move students from compliance to creativity, fostering deeper, more personal connections to learning.

When we honor multiple entry points into learning, we create space for more students to succeed. This approach reflects research from Renaissance Learning (2018), which found that when English learners access culturally appropriate and multi-modal instructional materials, their comprehension and participation increase substantially.

In the next sections, we'll explore how to:

Design lessons that center student identity and voice

Use literature as a launching point for inquiry, dialogue, and real-world connections

Differentiate responses to honor varied strengths and learning needs

Create assessments that measure more than just comprehension

Because planning with intention isn't just good teaching, it's how we make sure every student not only sees themselves in a book, but in the learning that follows.

Let's build lessons that do more than meet standards. Let's build lessons that matter.

Section Two: Designing Lessons That Center Identity and Voice

To design lessons that truly engage, we must begin by centering student identity and voice. This means creating opportunities for students to bring their whole selves into the learning process. When students see their culture, language, and lived experiences reflected in both the content and the structure of a lesson, they engage not only academically, but personally.

One approach is to embed identity reflection directly into literary analysis. Instead of simply asking for plot summaries or character traits, try prompts like: "How would this character be different if they came from your community?" or "What parts of this story remind you of your own experience?" These questions invite personal insight and validate each student's worldview.

Incorporating student voice also means allowing for choice in texts, in response formats, and in modes of expression. For example, students might choose between creating a podcast, writing a letter to a character, developing a short film scene, or composing a spoken word poem that reflects the story's theme. These are not gimmicks; they are invitations. Invitations for students to engage on their terms, using their strengths.

Research supports the power of this approach. The First Book (2023) Diverse Books Impact Study found that when students had voice and choice in the books they read and how they responded to them, they read more frequently and with greater interest. The NEA Foundation (2024) further emphasizes that culturally responsive teaching, which includes identity-affirming content and open-ended learning formats, improves academic achievement and strengthens classroom belonging.

Ultimately, designing lessons that center identity and voice transforms the classroom into a space of affirmation, agency, and deep connection. It reminds students that their perspectives are not just welcome, they are essential.

To begin designing these types of lessons in your own classroom, consider the following steps:

- Start with a culturally relevant text that resonates with your students' backgrounds or experiences.

- Create identity-based questions and prompts that link characters or themes to students' lived realities.

- Provide multiple avenues for response: visual, verbal, kinesthetic, and written.

- Co-create rubrics with students to reflect their values and voices.

- Make space for revision and dialogue, not just one-time responses.

This isn't about checking boxes. It's about co-creating meaning.

Section Four: Differentiating With Purpose

Differentiation is more than just offering a few choices or scaffolding a worksheet. True differentiation recognizes the whole child, their interests, cultural background, language development, social-emotional well-being, and the many ways they process and express learning. It's not about simplifying tasks for some and making them harder for others. It's about making sure every student has access to meaningful content in a way that honors who they are and how they learn.

To differentiate effectively, we must begin by knowing our students. Not just academically, but relationally. What excites them? What challenges do they carry into the classroom? How do they see themselves as learners? When we understand students' cultural identity, home context, emotional triggers, and self-perceptions, we can match our strategies to their real needs, not just their scores.

And here's the thing: differentiation isn't static. A student may need sentence frames one day and be ready to lead a discussion the next. Some students need more time. Others need a different path. We can't box students into one approach and call it differentiation. We have to remain responsive and flexible, which means embedding check-ins, conferencing, and reflective practice into our routines.

Carol Ann Tomlinson (2001), one of the leading scholars on differentiation, reminds us that we differentiate not only by content and product but also by process and learning environment. John Hattie's Visible Learning research affirms that differentiation has an effect size of 0.51, well above the threshold for strategies with significant impact on student growth. And when emotional safety and identity are considered as part of differentiation, students are more likely to feel empowered and included (Bradshaw et al., 2018).

I once worked with a student who was a fluent reader and demonstrated strong comprehension during class discussions. She could unpack metaphors, make brilliant text-to-world connections, and articulate themes with clarity. But when it came time for written assessments, something shifted. She would shut down, sometimes refusing to even pick up her pencil. When asked to write reflections or analysis, she'd simply stare at the page.

It wasn't about ability. It was about self-perception and emotional readiness. Through conferencing, I learned that she felt overwhelmed by the expectation of getting things "perfect" in writing. Her spoken brilliance wasn't translating to paper because of the pressure she placed on herself. So, we tried something different. I allowed her to record her reflections using a classroom tablet. Later, we worked together to transcribe her spoken thoughts into writing, gradually building her confidence.

This shift wasn't just about access, it was about affirmation. It said, "I see you. I believe in you. Let's find a way to help you shine."

Differentiation also opens the door for culturally sustaining pedagogy. When students are allowed to bring in their cultural knowledge, home language, and lived experiences, their learning deepens. Instead of asking all students to fit one mold, we celebrate the mosaic of ways students show brilliance.

To set up effective differentiation in your classroom:

- Conduct interest and learning profile surveys early in the year.
- Use flexible grouping based on task, readiness, or student-selected topics.
- Provide scaffolded resources such as sentence starters, graphic organizers, or translated materials based on current student needs.
- Adjust tasks for depth, not just quantity.
- Design activities that support multiple modalities (visual, auditory, kinesthetic).
- Build time for student reflection and goal-setting into your instructional cycle.

Differentiating with purpose ensures every student, not just the high flyers or the compliant, feels seen, supported, and capable. It says, "You matter here. We believe in your growth."

To design differentiated lessons that truly center student voice and needs, start with a strong culturally relevant text. Map out multiple entry points for the lesson, ensuring that students can interact with the material through writing, visuals, movement, and oral expression. Scaffold supports where needed and allow students to revise their work over time, reflecting on what they've learned and how they've grown. This kind of intentional design creates opportunities for success that feel personal, meaningful, and lasting.

Section Five: Building Bridges Through Formative Assessment

Effective lesson design doesn't end with the activity. It evolves with the learner. Formative assessments help educators monitor learning and adjust instruction in real time, but more importantly, they offer students a consistent sense of where they are, what they've mastered, and what still needs attention.

Yet, traditional assessments often miss the mark for students who think differently, communicate creatively, or process information through lived experience. When we rely solely on written responses, we may miss the brilliance of a student who can explain, debate, sketch, or build their understanding in alternative ways.

Creating an Effective Formative Assessment

Formative assessment should never feel like a "gotcha." Instead, it should feel like a mirror, a reflection of what students understand, what they're wrestling with, and where they feel confident. It's an ongoing dialogue between teacher and student, not a one-time snapshot. And like all meaningful conversations, it requires listening, noticing, and responding with care.

Start by asking: What do I want students to know, feel, and be able to do as a result of this lesson? From there, design your assessment with those goals in mind, keeping in mind multiple pathways for students to demonstrate their learning.

Here's a framework that I share with educators:

Clarify the Learning Intentions

Anchor your formative check-in to a clear goal. For example, if your objective is "Students will be able to identify and explain how a character's identity shapes their actions," make sure your assessment captures that, not just whether they can recall what happened in the story.

Use Varied Modalities

Offer different ways for students to show what they know:

Oral reflections (through partner talks or audio recordings)

Visual expressions (storyboards, sketchnotes, comic strips)

Performance (a monologue or reenactment)

Written reflections (short answer, journal entry, letter to a character)

According to research by Edutopia (2020), students demonstrate deeper understanding when they can choose how to express their knowledge, especially when that choice affirms their cultural and linguistic strengths.

Embed Feedback Loops

Assessment isn't assessment without feedback. Make time for peer feedback, teacher conferences, and student self-reflection. Encourage students to revise or extend their thinking after feedback is given. This supports a growth mindset and builds metacognitive skills.

Focus on Progress, Not Perfection

An effective formative assessment tracks growth, not just mastery. Use rubrics or checklists that value progress over product, such as "used textual evidence" or "made personal connection" rather than just correctness or completion.

Center Student Voice in Evaluation

Involve students in co-creating the success criteria. When students know what quality work looks like and have had a hand in defining it, they are more likely to strive for it and reflect on how to get there.

A helpful reminder from First Book's Diverse Books Impact Study (2023): when students see that their voices, choices, and cultures matter in the learning process, their motivation and sense of belonging rise significantly.

Say it with me: Assessment is a tool for learning, not a measure of worth. When done well, it's a bridge to understanding, not just of the content, but of our students themselves.

Section Six: Reflecting, Revising, and Rising

Every meaningful lesson doesn't just end with assessment, it ends with reflection. Not just from our students, but from us as educators. What worked? What needs adjustment? Who thrived? Who still needs support?

Reflection is the heartbeat of culturally responsive teaching. It's how we stay connected to our purpose and accountable to the students we serve. This isn't about self-critique for the sake of guilt; it's about growth. About listening with new ears and seeing with new eyes.

Let's begin with student reflection. After a lesson, ask students to reflect not just on what they learned, but how they felt during the learning process:

What did you enjoy?

What was challenging?

When did you feel most engaged?

Was there a moment you felt unseen or confused?

These types of reflective prompts are powerful. They help students practice metacognition, develop self-awareness, and build emotional literacy. According to the Collaborative for Academic, Social, and Emotional Learning (CASEL), students who regularly reflect and engage in self-assessment perform better academically and build stronger classroom relationships.

As educators, our reflection should include:

Did the lesson affirm my students' identities?

Were the learning goals met in ways that honored student voice and agency?

Did every student have access to success?

What will I try differently next time?

We also revise. Not out of failure, but with reflection. Just like our students, we grow with practice. One lesson might be too rigid. Another too open-ended. Sometimes the group dynamics surprise us. Sometimes a new insight from a student sparks a better way.

Consider keeping a teacher reflection journal or debriefing weekly with a colleague. Talk about the small wins and the missed opportunities. Celebrate what you tried even if it didn't go perfectly. Modeling this kind of reflective practice is an act of vulnerability and leadership.

And finally, we rise. We take the lessons we've learned, the reflections we've gathered, and the changes we've made, and we recommit. Recommit to designing with purpose. Recommit to knowing and honoring our students. Recommit to teaching in ways that heal and uplift.

Because every lesson we plan has the power to be more than a task. It can be a turning point. A mirror. A movement.

And it all begins with the willingness to reflect, revise, and rise.

References

Bradshaw, C. P., et al. (2018). [*Study on culturally responsive classroom strategies and student outcomes*]. [Full source details not provided in manuscript—recommend supplying publication/title for completion.]

Darling-Hammond, L. (2019). *The science of learning and development: Creating equitable and empowering learning environments.* Learning Policy Institute.

First Book. (2023). *Diverse Books Impact Study.* First Book Research & Insights.

NEA Foundation. (2024). *Culturally Responsive Teaching and Student Outcomes Report.* NEA Foundation.

Renaissance Learning. (2018). *What Kids Are Reading: 2018 edition.* Renaissance Learning.

Culture, it turns out, is the way that every brain makes sense of the world. That is why everyone, regardless of race or ethnicity, has a culture. Think of culture as software for the brain's hardware. The brain uses cultural information to turn everyday happenings into meaningful events. If we want to help dependent learners do more higher order thinking and problem solving, then we have to access their brain's cognitive structures to deliver culturally responsive instruction.

- Zaretta L. Hammond

Chapter Seven:

Responsive Teaching Practices That Center Students

Section One: Teaching With Presence, Not Perfection

Responsive teaching isn't about having the flashiest materials or the most polished delivery. It's about presence, the kind that listens deeply, adjusts thoughtfully, and places student identity and dignity at the center of every choice. According to Howard and Rodriguez (2021), schools that prioritize responsive dialogue and flexible teaching structures see stronger student-teacher relationships, fewer behavior referrals, and higher engagement.

Let's start here: your presence matters more than your perfection. Students remember how you made them feel—whether they were welcomed, heard, and valued. And that begins with intentional, student-centered practices that meet them where they are.

Try starting your day or lesson with a responsive check-in: a simple "What's one word that describes how you're feeling today?" followed by a journaling or partner share. These moments help ground the room and signal that emotional wellness is part of the learning process.

Research from the Learning Policy Institute (Darling-Hammond, 2019) emphasizes that emotional safety is a prerequisite for academic success. Students are more likely to participate, take risks, and persist through challenges when they feel emotionally secure in the classroom.

When we teach responsively, we make room for complexity, nuance, and real connection. We become co-learners, not just content deliverers.

Section Two: Inviting Every Voice Into the Room

Responsive classrooms are built on dialogue, not monologue. Yet in many traditional settings, a handful of students dominate classroom talk. The rest are watching the conversation happen around them.

That's where intentional structures come in. Strategies like Talking Circles, Think-Pair-Share, Silent Chalk Talks, and Four Corners invite broader participation and offer students multiple ways to enter the conversation.

I encourage you to try using a passing object during a talking circle—something meaningful, soft, or symbolic. I've seen quiet students come alive when it's their turn. One sixth grader who had never spoken aloud in class said, "It felt like my voice mattered for the first time."

Data from Banks et al. (2022) shows that when inclusive protocols were used consistently, multilingual student participation doubled within six weeks, and overall engagement rose by 34%.

When we invite every voice into the room, we're not just teaching content—we're building community.

Section Three: Creating Brave Spaces for Hard Conversations

Culturally relevant texts often bring complex, emotional truths into our classrooms. That's the power of literature, it invites honesty, perspective-taking, and sometimes discomfort. Responsive educators don't avoid these conversations. They prepare for them with care.

Start by co-creating classroom norms that emphasize curiosity, respect, and accountability. Phrases like "We speak from our experience," "We listen to understand," and "We repair when harm is done" are more than just posters. They are practices.

Could you imagine a high school teacher reimagining his classroom saying this?: "After reading *Stamped*, my students led a forum asking what our school needed to change. That conversation led to real policy revisions and deeper trust."

Yes, the data supports this. Schools using equity-based dialogue practices saw a 27% decrease in discipline referrals and increased student trust (Howard and Rodriguez, 2021).

Brave spaces are not perfect spaces. But they are places where truth, identity, and care coexist.

Section Four: Rethinking Assessment Through a Responsive Lens

Traditional assessments can miss the mark, especially for students whose brilliance doesn't fit neatly into standardized boxes. Responsive assessment honors student identity, voice, and growth. It asks, "How do you learn?" not just, "Did you get it right?"

Here are a few ways to make assessment more culturally and emotionally responsive:

Replace final essays with literary self-portraits, podcasts, or spoken word pieces.

Let students choose their response formats: visual, verbal, written, or performative.

Use rubrics that value growth, reflection, and personal connection, not just grammar and structure.

A teacher once told me: "When I let my students record their analysis instead of write it, I heard depth I'd never seen in their essays. It changed everything."

Martinez and Lee (2020) found that responsive assessments increase belonging by 41% and strengthen students' ability to articulate text-to-self connections.

Assessment should be a tool for empowerment, not a gatekeeper.

Section Five: Language That Heals, Not Harms

The way we speak to students becomes the voice they internalize. Responsive educators choose words that affirm, empower, and build bridges.

Instead of "You need to pay more attention," try: "What can we change to help you stay engaged?"

Instead of "That's inappropriate," ask: "What made you choose that response?"

Garcia and Monroe (2019) report that affirming feedback increases academic self-efficacy by nearly 20%. Students begin to believe in their capacity because their teachers reflect it back to them.

Even small shifts in language—like naming a student's strength before offering a correction—can transform the tone of a classroom. Responsive language says: "I see you. I believe in you. Let's grow together."

Section Six: Reflecting and Reimagining in Real Time

The most responsive classrooms are not built overnight. They evolve through trial, reflection, and adaptation. That's the beauty of this work, it's living, breathing, and always in motion.

Reflection isn't just for students. Ask yourself:

Did my lesson affirm identity?

Did I make space for all voices?

Who thrived today, and who didn't?

What might I try differently next time?

Consider keeping a reflection journal or voice memo after your lessons. Celebrate what went well. Get curious about what didn't. Invite feedback from students. When we model growth, our students learn to embrace it, too.

Darling-Hammond (2019) reminds us: responsive teaching is less about mastery and more about mindset. The mindset that says: "I don't have to know everything. I just have to keep learning."

So let's teach with that kind of presence. Let's co-create classrooms that reflect, respond, and rise with our students.

Because responsive teaching isn't an extra thing. It's the heart of everything.

References

Banks, R., Nguyen, T., & Patel, S. *Equity in Dialogue: A Multischool Study on Engagement and Participation.* Urban Learning Press, 2022.

Darling-Hammond, L. *The Science of Learning and Development: Creating Equitable and Empowering Learning Environments.* Learning Policy Institute, 2019.

Garcia, R., & Monroe, T. *The Language of Belonging: Feedback That Fosters Student Identity.* Journal of Equitable Practices, vol. 11, no. 3, 2019, pp. 33–46.

Howard, T., & Rodriguez, C. *Restorative Conversations and School Culture: Practical Applications for Equity.* Teachers for Justice Journal, vol. 18, no. 2, 2021, pp. 44–57.

Martinez, J., & Lee, A. *Beyond the Test: Culturally Sustaining Assessments in the Middle Grades.* Learning Equity Review, vol. 5, no. 1, 2020, pp. 12–27.

Chapter Eight:

Opportunities for Student Voice

Section One: The Power of Voice in Learning

When students have opportunities to express themselves, to be heard, and to shape their learning, something shifts. The classroom becomes more than a place where knowledge is delivered. It becomes a space of co-creation, of agency, of ownership. Student voice is not a bonus or an enrichment activity. It is a central part of equity-centered, culturally responsive teaching.

According to The First Book (2023) Diverse Books Impact Study, when students are given opportunities to lead discussions, design projects, or respond to literature in ways that reflect their experiences, their engagement increases significantly. This matters. Because when students are invited to speak from their lived realities, they begin to see themselves not just as learners but as contributors.

Creating opportunities for student voice begins with a mindset shift. It requires educators to move from being the sole authority in the room to becoming facilitators, listeners, and co-learners. This does not mean lowering expectations. It means raising the bar for authenticity, creativity, and connection.

Section Two: Storytelling as a Gateway

One of the most powerful ways to center student voice is through storytelling. When students are encouraged to share their own stories, whether in writing, audio, video, or visual art, they begin to understand the value of their perspectives.

Start by creating space for students to connect the literature they read to their own lives. Instead of asking only comprehension questions, ask reflective ones like:

What in this story reminds you of your own experience?

If you were to write a version of this story from your perspective, what would it include?

When these prompts are offered consistently, students begin to develop confidence in their ability to connect personally and critically to texts. This can open the door to projects such as personal essays, digital storytelling, podcasts, or memoir writing.

In classrooms where storytelling is centered, it is possible that a student who has struggled to participate in traditional writing assignments may feel empowered to share their story through a recorded audio journal. Another student might express deep connection to a novel's theme through a spoken word piece, revealing insights that might never surface in a quiz.

Section Three: Choice as a Catalyst for Voice

Providing choice is one of the simplest and most effective ways to honor student voice. This can include choice in texts, assignments, response formats, or group roles. When students have options, they are more likely to invest in the work and bring more of themselves into the process.

In practice, this might look like offering students three text options for a literature circle, each one reflecting different cultures, themes, or genres. Or, after finishing a novel, students might choose whether to write a character diary, create a spoken word response, or design a visual representation of a theme.

When meaningful choices are built into the learning process, students may begin to explore new ways of expressing understanding. For example, a multilingual student might choose to create a bilingual children's book based on a theme from the novel, showcasing both literacy and cultural pride. Another student might design a short animation to visually capture a character's internal conflict.

This type of choice supports autonomy and builds decision-making skills. It allows students to lean into their strengths and interests. Research from the NEA Foundation (2024) shows that student choice in how they engage with literature leads to higher completion rates, more thoughtful responses, and greater persistence.

Section Four: Inquiry-Driven Projects

Student voice also flourishes through inquiry. When students are given the chance to ask big questions and investigate issues that matter to them, they begin to take learning personally. This moves beyond traditional research papers into passion-driven exploration.

Literature can serve as a launching point. A text that addresses immigration, for example, might lead students to explore their own family's migration stories or to examine current events in their local community. A book that explores environmental justice might inspire students to investigate pollution in their neighborhood and propose solutions.

In a classroom rooted in inquiry, students may decide to research food deserts in their city after reading a novel set in an under-resourced community. Another group might design an awareness campaign around housing justice, using themes from a class novel as a foundation.

Inquiry-based learning positions students as experts in the making. It tells them, your questions matter. Your insights matter. Your curiosity is valid. According to Darling-Hammond (2019), inquiry-based instruction builds critical thinking skills and promotes deeper learning across disciplines.

Section Five: Making Space for Student-Led Discussion

Student voice thrives in classrooms where dialogue is shared. This means creating consistent opportunities for students to lead discussions, ask questions, and respond to each other, not just to the teacher.

Protocols like Socratic Seminars, fishbowl discussions, or peer-facilitated literature circles can help shift ownership of the conversation. These structures work best when they are introduced early, practiced regularly, and refined through feedback.

In a student-led discussion, one might see students using discussion stems to challenge or build on a peer's ideas. A student may step into the facilitator role and prompt the group with, "How does this chapter challenge what we thought we knew about the character?" Another may document peer insights in a discussion tracker and synthesize them into a collaborative blog post.

The goal is not just to increase talk time. It is to build habits of respectful dialogue, perspective-taking, and shared meaning-making.

Section Six: Voice in Evaluation and Feedback

If we want student voice to be authentic, we need to invite it into our systems of evaluation as well. This means offering students opportunities to reflect on their learning, co-create rubrics, and give feedback on classroom practices.

Ask students:

What kind of feedback helps you grow?

What would you change about this assignment?

What do you want me to understand about how you learn?

Classroom scenarios might include students working in groups to design a rubric for a creative project, then using it to assess their own and peers' work. A reflection journal might include student responses to prompts like, "What are you most proud of in this unit?" or "How did your identity shape the way you responded to the text?"

Research from Martinez and Lee (2020) shows that when students co-design success criteria and reflect regularly on their progress, their sense of agency and academic confidence grows.

Voice in evaluation helps create classrooms that are more equitable, transparent, and responsive.

Because when we make room for student voice, we do more than hear what students think. We affirm who they are. We remind them that their thoughts, stories, and insights matter, not just for school, but for the world beyond it.

References

Darling-Hammond, L. *The Science of Learning and Development: Creating Equitable and Empowering Learning Environments.* Learning Policy Institute, 2019.

First Book. *Diverse Books Impact Study.* 2023.

Martinez, J., & Lee, A. *Beyond the Test: Culturally Sustaining Assessments in the Middle Grades.* Learning Equity Review, vol. 5, no. 1, 2020, pp. 12–27.

NEA Foundation. *Culturally Responsive Teaching and Student Outcomes Report.* 2024.

Chapter Nine:

Reimagine the System

Section One: Systems Hold Stories

Curriculum is more than content. It is a mirror of what we value, who we center, and what narratives we believe are worth telling. When we take a closer look at the systems that shape our classrooms, district policies, state standards, curriculum maps, and pacing guides, we begin to see that they are not neutral. These structures were designed with a specific worldview, often one that prioritizes dominant cultural norms while marginalizing or erasing others.

To reimagine the system, we must begin with honesty. Many of the educational systems we've inherited were not created for all students to thrive. In fact, they often operate in ways that disproportionately benefit some students while systematically excluding others. According to the Cooperative Children's Book Center (2023), more than 70 percent of children's books published in the United States continue to center white characters. If the stories students see in books are this limited, imagine the representation or lack thereof, in assessments, curriculum pacing guides, and instructional resources.

Reimagining the system means asking bold questions: Who designed these structures? Who continues to benefit from them? Who is being left behind? And how do we change that—not just in individual classrooms, but across entire schools and districts?

Section Two: Auditing Curriculum With Purpose

A curriculum audit is one of the most powerful tools a school or district can use to examine equity. It is not about blame. It is about naming patterns and making informed, intentional decisions that align with our values.

To start, gather a team that includes teachers, coaches, administrators, and ideally students and families. Review the texts, authors, themes, and standards that shape your curriculum. Use tools such as equity rubrics or text analysis guides to examine the following:

Whose voices and stories are being told?

Who is consistently portrayed in deficit-based or stereotypical roles?

Are there authors of color represented across grade levels, not just in isolated months or units?

Do students see themselves reflected in texts that center joy, brilliance, and complexity?

A school might map core texts by demographic data, topic, publication year, and connection to student identity. From there, the team can identify gaps and set short- and long-term goals for improvement. This process could lead to the adoption of new texts, the revision of existing units, or the inclusion of supplemental materials that broaden perspectives.

This is not about discarding literature. It is about making room for what has long been missing. Representation in curriculum must be proactive, not performative.

Section Three: Embedding Equity Into Professional Learning

Professional learning must go beyond strategies and toolkits. It must begin with identity, reflection, and a commitment to anti-bias work. Educators cannot teach what they have not wrestled with. That means creating ongoing spaces for adults to examine their own experiences, beliefs, and blind spots.

Effective equity-centered professional development includes:

Facilitated sessions that explore identity, culture, and privilege

Book studies focused on racial equity, culturally sustaining pedagogy, or critical literacy

Coaching cycles that align instructional goals with culturally responsive practices

Use of student feedback and classroom artifacts to inform professional growth

Leadership teams can support this work by modeling it themselves. When principals and coaches engage in reflection and share their learning, they create a culture where growth is expected, not optional.

A district might create a year-long professional learning arc that begins with identity mapping, moves into bias awareness, and connects to inclusive instructional design. This type of intentional design helps ensure that equity is not a theme for one workshop but a thread that runs through the fabric of the school year.

Section Four: Shifting the Role of Instructional Leadership

Instructional leadership must evolve to support teachers who are doing the deep work of equity. Leaders have the power to shift what is prioritized and protected. That begins with how we observe, coach, and evaluate.

Instead of walkthroughs focused on pacing or compliance, consider designing equity-focused look-fors. These might include:

Evidence of student voice in classroom discussion

Use of culturally relevant texts or materials

Strategies that support multilingual learners or neurodiverse students

Opportunities for student identity to be reflected in assignments and assessments

Coaching conversations can also shift. Rather than asking, "Did you meet your objective?" consider asking, "How did this lesson affirm your students' identities?" or "Where did students show ownership of their learning?"

When leaders prioritize these types of questions, they signal to teachers that culturally responsive teaching is not an extra. It is essential. And when that happens, educators feel more empowered to take instructional risks that center their students.

Section Five: Creating Space for Student Partnership

Students must be part of the work of reimagining systems. Too often, school improvement conversations happen without the very people most affected by them. Yet students bring insight, experience, and creativity that can transform how we teach and lead.

To bring student voice into system change:

Form student curriculum review councils

Include student representatives in instructional leadership teams

Create feedback loops through surveys, listening sessions, or interviews

Students can offer input on what texts feel relevant, how classroom environments support or hinder belonging, and what changes would make learning more meaningful. Imagine students helping revise a school's summer reading list to include stories that reflect the community's diversity. Or contributing to a rubric that evaluates the inclusiveness of a classroom library.

When students see that their voice matters at the system level, they begin to believe in their own capacity to lead.

Section Six: Policies That Reflect Our Commitments

For equity to live beyond intentions, it must be embedded in policy. Schools and districts can adopt formal language and processes that ensure representation, relevance, and responsiveness are not left to chance.

Consider developing or revising policies that:

Set standards for inclusive text selection and curriculum adoption

Require ongoing professional development tied to equity outcomes

Include student belonging and engagement metrics in school improvement plans

Embed equity goals into teacher evaluation and instructional coaching protocols

When policies reflect our equity commitments, we create sustainability. We make sure this work is not dependent on individual champions or one-time initiatives.

For example, a district might revise its textbook adoption process to include a review panel that evaluates materials for cultural relevance and identity affirmation. Or a school might include equity walkthroughs as part of its leadership team's monthly responsibilities.

Policy is how we move from belief to practice. From vision to structure. From hoping for change to building it.

Because reimagining the system is not about tearing everything down. It is about redesigning with purpose. It is about creating schools where every child is seen, affirmed, and equipped to thrive, not by accident, but by design.

References

Cooperative Children's Book Center. *Books by and About Black, Indigenous and People of Color 2023.* University of Wisconsin–Madison, 2023.

NEA Foundation. *Culturally Responsive Teaching and Student Outcomes Report.* 2024.

Chapter Ten:

What Culturally relevant Literature Looks Like

Section One: More Than a "Diverse" Book

Culturally relevant literature is not just about featuring characters of color, translating a few texts, or including one story about a different culture during a heritage month. It is about recognizing literature as a tool for identity affirmation, critical consciousness, and human connection.

To be culturally relevant, a book must do more than diversify the bookshelf. It must challenge dominant narratives, affirm the cultural assets of students, and open up space for critical dialogue. These texts must reflect and respect the lived experiences of students while offering new perspectives that push thinking.

Books that are often labeled "diverse" are sometimes chosen without deeper analysis. A text that features a character of color but is rooted in trauma or stereotype can cause harm. We must ask deeper questions about our selections:

Does this text affirm the beauty and complexity of the culture it portrays?

Are the characters fully developed with agency, not simply reactive or tragic?

Who wrote this story, and for whom was it written?

How will this book make my students feel seen, valued, or provoked to think critically?

Reflective Questions:

When you choose texts, what criteria guide your decisions?

How often do students see themselves as main characters in the stories you teach?

Are the "diverse" books in your collection centered in joy, or only trauma?

Section Two: Texts That Invite Connection

Connection is the heartbeat of engagement. Culturally relevant literature offers students a way to say, "This story understands me." When students encounter books that reflect their identities, values, or home languages, their participation often shifts from compliance to curiosity.

These texts validate students' lives and experiences. A book that includes Spanish dialogue without italicizing it signals respect for bilingualism. A story set in an urban neighborhood that avoids deficit framing can help a student feel proud of where they're from. When students recognize themselves in literature, the classroom becomes a place where their existence is not questioned, it is celebrated.

These connections also build bridges between students. When a classroom reads a book that reflects the identity of one student, it affirms that student and educates others. Everyone grows.

Reflective Questions:

What stories in your curriculum might reflect a student's home language, traditions, or community?

What conversations have emerged when students personally connect with a text?

How can you use texts to build empathy and understanding across differences?

Section Three: The Power of Joy-Based Texts

Culturally relevant literature must include narratives of resistance, but it must also include narratives of joy, love, celebration, and everyday life. When we only offer stories of trauma, we risk reinforcing the idea that students' identities are always connected to suffering.

Joy-based texts remind students that their cultures and communities are sources of pride, laughter, creativity, and strength. These stories can be especially powerful in shifting perceptions for students who are used to seeing themselves only through the lens of struggle.

Think about what it means for a Black boy to see a superhero who shares his skin tone, or for a Muslim girl to read about a character who finds joy in her traditions. These moments affirm dignity.

Reflective Questions:

How many of the texts you use center joy for historically marginalized communities?

What messages are students internalizing about themselves through the stories they read?

How might your students define "representation" if you asked them?

Section Four: Text Makeovers

Relevance is not only about adding new texts. It is also about transforming the way we teach existing ones. A "text makeover" invites educators to reframe a traditional book through a more inclusive, critical lens.

This might involve:

- Pairing a canonical text with a contemporary counter-narrative
- Adding essential questions that explore power, voice, and identity
- Asking students to imagine untold stories of minoritized characters
- Exploring how historical context influences the author's perspective

For example, when teaching *To Kill a Mockingbird*, educators can introduce primary sources on racial justice, invite students to analyze the narrative voice, and compare the novel with contemporary works by Black authors who write about justice and resistance on their own terms.

Reflective Questions:

What traditional texts do you teach that could benefit from a cultural lens?

How might you create space for students to question or challenge the dominant narrative?

What other voices could you bring into the unit to add depth and complexity?

Section Five: Cross-Content Connections

Culturally relevant literature does not belong to the ELA classroom alone. In fact, some of the richest learning happens when students see their identities and histories valued across subjects.

In social studies, pairing primary texts with memoirs can illuminate personal perspectives on historical events. In science, reading about scientists from diverse backgrounds can inspire underrepresented students to see themselves in STEM fields. In art or music, stories can inspire student creations that reflect cultural heritage.

These cross-content connections also allow students to apply critical thinking skills in multiple contexts. They begin to understand that identity, culture, and power show up everywhere—not just in stories, but in data, design, and daily life.

Reflective Questions:

How can you partner with colleagues to embed culturally relevant texts across content areas?

What interdisciplinary themes could unify your teaching team's work?

How can students explore identity, culture, and justice across subjects?

Section Six: Bringing Texts to Life

When culturally relevant texts come alive in the classroom, they become more than content. They become catalysts. Catalysts for creativity, conversation, community, and confidence.

Students can bring these texts to life by:

Creating podcast episodes reflecting on key themes

Designing visual art inspired by a character's journey

Hosting community storytelling nights featuring literature they love

Writing and performing monologues from alternate perspectives

These activities deepen comprehension and provide authentic audiences for student work. They also allow students to explore their identities in affirming ways.

Imagine students creating a collaborative mural after reading a book about neighborhood activism, or recording multilingual book reviews to share with younger students. These projects shift the classroom from a place of passive consumption to one of creative contribution.

Reflective Questions:

What opportunities do students have to respond to literature creatively?

How can student projects reach audiences beyond the classroom?

What texts might inspire students to tell their own stories?

Because culturally relevant literature is not just what we teach—it is how we honor the voices, identities, and brilliance of the students in front of us.

References

Darling-Hammond, L. (2019). *The science of learning and development: Creating equitable and empowering learning environments.* Learning Policy Institute.

Hattie, J. (2009). *Visible learning: A synthesis of over 800 meta-analyses relating to achievement.* Routledge.

Tomlinson, C. A. (2017). *The differentiated classroom: Responding to the needs of all learners (2nd ed.).* ASCD.

Chapter Eleven:

Planning Engaging Lessons With Impact

Section One: Where Intention Meets Practice

Representation in literature is a powerful beginning, but it cannot end there. Culturally relevant teaching calls us to go beyond choosing the right books and into the deeper work of designing learning experiences that center student identity, voice, and agency.

According to the NEA Foundation (2024), students engage more deeply with literature when lessons reflect their lived experiences and invite them to think critically about the world around them. In other words, the right book is the spark, but it is the lesson that fans the flame.

This means moving away from compliance-based instruction and toward intentional, identity-affirming lesson design. When educators design with cultural relevance in mind, they honor not just what students know, but who they are.

Lessons should be structured to affirm students' backgrounds, create space for multiple perspectives, and challenge dominant narratives. They should also include multiple ways for students to respond because engagement is not one size fits all.

Reflective Questions:

In your most recent unit, whose experiences and ways of knowing were centered?

How often do students have opportunities to shape or extend the lesson?

Are your learning outcomes focused on student voice, reflection, and connection, or just compliance?

Section Two: Designing Lessons That Center Identity and Voice

To design lessons that engage, educators must begin with students at the center, not the standard or the pacing guide. Centering identity means creating space for students to bring their whole selves into the learning process.

Start by asking: What identities, cultures, or lived experiences do my students bring? How might this lesson invite them to connect, contribute, and feel seen?

Rather than asking students to write summaries or analyze character traits, try prompts that explore self and story:

How does this character's experience mirror or differ from yours?

What does this story make you think or feel about your own identity?

What questions does this text raise about the world we live in?

Offering choice in texts, formats, and discussion modes is another powerful way to honor voice. Students might respond through poetry, podcasting, artwork, or open letters. These options are not just about creativity; they are about access and affirmation.

Reflective Questions:

What opportunities exist for students to connect their identity to the content?

How often are students asked to reflect on or share their perspectives?

Do all students have access points to feel seen and heard in your lessons?

Section Three: Using Literature as a Launching Point

Books are not the end goal. They are the beginning. A culturally relevant text opens the door to inquiry, dialogue, and exploration.

Ask yourself: What conversations does this book make possible? What questions might students ask about justice, belonging, or identity after reading this text?

For example, reading a novel about displacement could launch a local research project on migration stories. A picture book about neighborhood resilience might lead to a community mapping activity. A poem about language and power could inspire a multilingual celebration of student voice.

Build your lessons around essential questions that help students connect the learning to their own lives and explore ideas together as a class. Questions like:

Whose stories are missing, and why?

How does this story connect to issues we see in our own community?

What does this text teach us about power, identity, or resistance?

Reflective Questions:

Do your lessons move beyond the text to connect with real-world issues?

Are students invited to explore, question, and build on what they read?

What kind of impact do you want the text to have on students' thinking and lives?

Section Four: Differentiating With Purpose

Differentiation in culturally responsive classrooms is not just about scaffolding skills. It is about honoring different ways of knowing, processing, and expressing learning. ifferentiation should not be mistaken for reducing expectations, nor for simply adding more work for gifted students; rather, it is about reimagining learning experiences in meaningful ways.

Begin by getting to know your students deeply: their linguistic assets, learning preferences, cultural identities, and past school experiences. Then, use that knowledge to create multiple pathways to success.

For example:

Offer sentence starters, translated materials, or visual supports for multilingual learners.

Allow oral storytelling, sketching, or performance as valid forms of analysis.

Use interest-based grouping for collaborative projects that highlight student strengths.

Differentiation must also include space for emotional readiness. A student who has experienced trauma may need alternative ways to engage with texts that reflect difficult topics. Honor their needs without excluding them from the learning.

Reflective Questions:

How do your scaffolds support, not simplify, student thinking?

Are your differentiation strategies rooted in equity or convenience?

How do you respond when a student needs a different path to engage fully?

Section Five: Building Bridges Through Formative Assessment

Assessment should never be a trap. It should be a mirror, a tool that reflects growth, invites reflection, and honors the journey.

In culturally responsive classrooms, formative assessment is woven throughout instruction. It shows up as student self-reflection, peer feedback, creative expression, and teacher conferencing. It values voice and process over perfection.

Use formative assessment to check not only what students know, but how they are thinking and feeling. Consider:

- Quick writes or journals with reflection prompts
- Audio or video reflections instead of written responses
- Sketch notes or storyboards for comprehension checks

And most importantly, use what you learn to adjust instruction. Responsive teaching means responsive assessment.

Reflective Questions:

What does your assessment say about what you value in student learning?

How often do students reflect on their growth, not just their grade?

How do you use formative data to change course, slow down, or go deeper?

Section Six: Reflecting, Revising, and Rising

Every lesson, no matter how well planned, is an invitation to learn. Not just for students, but for educators too. Culturally responsive teaching is not static. It grows with you.

After every lesson or unit, pause and reflect:

Who thrived in this lesson, and why?

Who struggled to connect, and what might I try differently?

Did this lesson affirm identity, promote inquiry, and foster voice?

Use student feedback as a compass. Create space for students to share what worked, what could change, and how they experienced the learning. Their insights can guide your revisions in ways you might not expect.

And remember: growth is the goal, not perfection. Every revision you make is an act of care. Every reflection is a recommitment to the students you serve.

Reflective Questions:

What do your lesson reflections reveal about your teaching values?

How often do you revise based on student feedback or outcomes?

What is one thing you can do tomorrow to better center your students?

Because planning with intention is not just good teaching. It is how we make sure every student not only sees themselves in a book, but in the learning that follows.

References

Brown-Jeffy, S., & Cooper, J. E. (2011). *Toward a conceptual framework of culturally relevant pedagogy: An overview of the conceptual and theoretical literature. Teacher Education Quarterly, 38(1), 65–84.*

Gay, G. (2018). *Culturally responsive teaching: Theory, research, and practice (3rd ed.).* Teachers College Press.

Ladson-Billings, G. (1995). *Toward a theory of culturally relevant pedagogy.* American Educational Research Journal, 32(3), 465–491.

Students are not blank slates. They enter the classroom with diverse experiences. Teachers should encourage students to draw on their prior knowledge in order to contribute to group discussions, which provides an anchor to learning. Taking a different approach to the literature that's taught in classrooms is one example of this.

- Cherese Childers-McKee

Lesson Planning Templates and Supporting Materials

These flexible planning templates are designed to help educators bring to life the concepts from Chapters 6–11 of Every Child Deserves a Mirror. Each section aligns with a key chapter and includes prompts, scaffolds, and guiding questions to support culturally relevant, identity-affirming instruction.

Chapter 6:
Planning Engaging Lessons With Impact
Identity-Centered Lesson Planning Template

1. Learning Objective (Academic + Identity Goal):

What do I want students to know, understand, or do? What do I want them to reflect on or see in themselves?

_____

_____

_____

_____

_____

_____

2. Essential Question(s):

Open-ended, student-facing questions that invite reflection, connection, and inquiry.

_____

_____

_____

_____

_____

_____

3. Text(s) Used:

Culturally relevant book(s), multimedia, or student-generated text.

_____

_____

_____

_____

_____

_____

_____

_____

4. Identity + Voice Integration:

What parts of the lesson center student voice or experience?

_____

_____

_____

_____

_____

_____

How will students explore their own identity?

_____
_____
_____
_____
_____

5. Lesson Activity:

Engaging task or experience that connects literature to lived experience.

_____
_____
_____

6. Creative Response Options:

E.g., visual journal, audio reflection, open letter, digital story.

_____
_____
_____
_____
_____
_____

7. Assessment for Understanding + Growth:

How will I know what students are learning AND how they're processing it?

_____
_____
_____
_____
_____
_____
_____
_____
_____

8. Student Reflection Prompt:

What did you see, feel, or realize today?

_____
_____
_____
_____
_____
_____

Chapter 7:
Responsive Teaching Practices
Responsive Teaching Reflection and Planning Tool

1. Discussion Structures:

☐ Think-Pair-Share

☐ Talking Circle

☐ Fishbowl

☐ Student-led Seminar

2. Voice Equity Plan:

Who usually speaks? Who is quiet? How will I shift that pattern?

_____

_____

_____

_____

_____

_____

_____

_____

3. Difficult Conversations Framework:

- Agreements for dialogue
- Pause and Repair strategies
- Reflection spaces for processing

4. Responsive Assessment Options:

☐ Oral explanation

☐ Podcast

☐ One-on-one conference

☐ Visual demonstration

☐ Self-assessment journal

5. Emotional Readiness Checks:

Quick prompts: How are you feeling about today's topic?

_____

_____

_____

_____

_____

What do you need?

_____

_____

_____

_____

_____

Chapter 8:
Opportunities for Student Voice
Student Voice Integration Planner

1. What parts of this lesson allow for student choice or leadership?

☐ Text selection

☐ Format of response

☐ Group roles

☐ Project design

2. Storytelling or Identity Work:

What opportunities exist for students to share their personal narratives?

_____

_____

_____

_____

_____

_____

_____

_____

_____

3. Inquiry + Research Invitations:

What questions can students explore based on the text or theme?

_____
_____
_____
_____
_____
_____
_____
_____
_____
_____
_____
_____
_____

4. Student Feedback Loop:

- End-of-lesson reflection
- Mid-unit check-in survey
- Peer and teacher co-assessment

Chapter 9:
Reimagining the System
Mini Curriculum Equity Audit Template

1. Current Core Texts:

List of titles by grade level or course.

_____   _____

_____   _____

_____   _____

_____   _____

_____   _____

2. Audit Questions:

Who is represented as the hero or narrator?

_____

_____

_____

_____

What themes are repeated? Whose histories are missing?

_____

_____

_____

Are there opportunities for joy, complexity, and nuance?

_____
_____
_____
_____
_____
_____
_____
_____
_____
_____
_____
_____

3. Author + Character Identity Tracking:

Book/Author: _____

Race/Ethnicity: ☐ African American ☐ Latinx ☐ Asian ☐ Indigenous ☐ White ☐ Other _____

Gender: ☐ Male ☐ Female ☐ Non-binary ☐ Other _____

Language: ☐ English ☐ Spanish ☐ Other _____

Region: _____

Cultural Affiliation: _____

***

Book/Author: _____

Race/Ethnicity: ☐ African American ☐ Latinx ☐ Asian ☐ Indigenous ☐ White ☐ Other _____

Gender: ☐ Male ☐ Female ☐ Non-binary ☐ Other _____

Language: ☐ English ☐ Spanish ☐ Other _____

Region: _____

Cultural Affiliation: _____

***

Book/Author: _____

Race/Ethnicity: ☐ African American ☐ Latinx ☐ Asian ☐ Indigenous ☐ White ☐ Other _____

Gender: ☐ Male ☐ Female ☐ Non-binary ☐ Other _____

Language: ☐ English ☐ Spanish ☐ Other _____

Region: _____

Cultural Affiliation: _____

4. Next Steps:

☐ Add new texts

☐ Revise existing units

☐ Create companion materials

☐ Engage students in audit process

Chapter 10:
What Culturally relevant Literature Looks Like
Text Selection + Reflection Tool

1. Title:

_____

_____

2. Author Identity + Intent:

_____

_____

3. Cultural Relevance Checklist:

☐ Reflects student identities

☐ Avoids stereotypes

☐ Includes joy and complexity

☐ Written by someone from the culture represented

☐ Encourages reflection, connection, or inquiry

4. Use in Curriculum:

Unit Theme:_____

_____

_____

Paired Texts:_____

_____

Student Reflection Prompt:_____

_____
_____
_____
_____
_____
_____
_____
_____
_____
_____
_____
_____
_____

5. Classroom Possibilities:

☐ Storytelling project
☐ Visual response
☐ Community interview
☐ Text pairing with current event

Chapter 11:
Planning Engaging Lessons With Impact
Culturally Responsive Lesson Design Framework

1. Student-Centered Learning Goals:

Academic learning target:_____

_____

_____

Identity or voice-based goal:_____

_____

_____

2. Connection to Text or Theme:

How does this lesson use literature or storytelling to deepen connection?

_____

_____

_____

_____

_____

_____

_____

_____

3. Essential Questions for Reflection and Action:

What does this text help us see or question?

_____

_____

_____

_____

_____

How does it connect to our lives, communities, or identities?

_____

_____

_____

_____

_____

4. Culturally Responsive Strategies Used:

☐ Identity exploration
☐ Inquiry-based learning
☐ Creative expression
☐ Choice and flexibility
☐ Culturally affirming scaffolds

5. Modes of Engagement:

☐ Discussion protocols

☐ Artistic response

☐ Project-based learning

☐ Multimedia creation

☐ Movement or roleplay

6. Formative Assessment + Feedback:

How will I monitor growth?

_____

_____

_____

_____

_____

_____

How will students reflect on their learning?

_____

_____

_____

_____

_____

_____

7. Reflection and Revision:

What worked well?

_____
_____
_____
_____
_____
_____

What surprised me?

_____
_____
_____
_____
_____
_____

How did students show up and engage?

_____
_____
_____
_____

What would I adapt next time?

_____

_____

_____

_____

_____

_____

_____

_____

_____

_____

_____

_____

_____

_____

_____

_____

_____

_____

_____

_____

These tools are meant to evolve with your students. Use them as starting points to co-design lessons, reflect on your choices, and build a classroom where every student's story is seen, valued, and centered.